Pricing Your Services

CREATING BENCHMARKS FOR YOUR SALON

&

DEVELOPING A PROFITABLE BONUS SYSTEM

The definitive guide to pricing your salon services
and controlling your profit margin

Foreward

Since 1997 I have been presenting my Keynote, "Pricing your services". The evolution and expansion from discussion to book, comes as a result of many years of experience as a business manager and through the enthusiasm of my wife, family, friends and colleagues. I have debated with my peers and educated myself on this topic during many late nights and in-depth conversations. The sharing of ideas and thoughts, over my years of involvement in the hairdressing and beauty industry has truely opened my mind.

Countless friends, colleagues and family members have thrown their ideas "into the mix". This has resulted in the publishing of this book and the development of our two Apps.

The ability to access "up to the minute" cost calculation, and the knowledge to plan a price strategy for your business is fundamental to your salon's success.

Until now the majority of salon owners had only their competitors price to use as a guide when pricing the services in their salon.

In a market that has been de-regulated, and where oversupply has caused self doubt and diminished prices, it is essential that accurate information regarding your expenses and profit margin is on hand instantaneously.

Many thanks must go to the support, knowledge and encouragement of my wife, the assistance with editing from some great friends and the skills of our app developer.

I am hoping that the information contained in this book and the ease of calculation provided by the App, will be a useful tool for all owners and managers who struggle to make a profit from their business on a daily basis.

THE OVERVIEW

Since the late 1990's, I have had the pleasure, as well as the frustration of working with hundreds of Salons Owners. They have shared their aspirations, ideas and concerns with me. They all have, a desperate desire to make their business profitable. Being profitable, became even more difficult when the hairdressing industry was de-regulated. You might wonder, why I would decide to write a book about pricing? Doesn't everyone know how to set there prices? Sadly, the answer is, they have no idea. Of course, they know how to SET their prices, but the problem of profitability arises because, they have never been taught how too CALCULATE, the price they NEED to make a profit. If this calculation is even slightly inaccurate, they will never reach their targets, and never ever make a reasonable profit.

The underlying tone, is nearly always the same, there is a real desire to "look after" their team, nearly always, they attempt to pay above award wages, and use poorly calculated bonus schemes, even when the real income target is rarely reached, this inevitably leaves the Salon owner out of pocket, and with little or no profit. The other concern, most salon owners agonise over, is for the welfare of the their clients, these owners, go through intense soul searching, when faced with the need to raise their prices, even if the price rise is as little as 2 or $3. In spite of the poor profits, and continuous worry, these Salon Owners push on with their goals. I have truly been inspired by many of these wonderful people, sometimes, almost to the point of tears. My decision to write this book comes from a simple desire to see reward for effort, my hope is that the "Pricing your Services" Program will provide a vehicle for salon owners to take charge of their businesses, and that they will be able to achieve their dreams, for themselves, their team, and their clients.

I felt the pain. When I bought my first Salon Business, I made some terribly incorrect assumptions. These assumptions have haunted my profit line for a number of years. These errors took me a while to overcome, and, the more I turned for advice within the hairdressing industry, the more I realised, that none of them had ever been instructed on how to calculate their cost plus margin price. None of them, had any idea of the "market price model" or "perceived value pricing."

I made three incorrect assumptions. Firstly, and most stupidly, I assumed, the owners of the large established hair salons and franchises, and the award winning hairdressers, knew what they were doing. I believed, that through years of accurate price calculation these highly praised, and apparently successful businesses, had arrived at the premium price for their services. Secondly, I assumed, that the majority of clients shopped around, and compared the prices of all of the salons in their area, then chose the lowest priced salon. Then another group of wealthy clients, from wealthy suburbs, went to expensive salons, because those salons had won hairdressing awards, and possessed highly skilled staff.

The third, and most incorrect assumption I made, was, the belief that, "I," knew the price, each client was willing to pay for their hairdressing services. It is only recently that have I realised, that like myself, many salons owners have been plagued by making similar decisions, based on the guesswork of others.

To set your picture straight, let's start from the beginning, and review our business approach. Think carefully about the following questions. Are you a Hairdresser who has their own hairdressing salon? Or, are you a Business Person who operates a hairdressing business? Depending on your answer, the focus and direction of your business will vary significantly. The pricing strategy and structure of your business, will also vary enormously. Whilst there is no correct answer, and the path chosen is entirely up to you, your ultimate success depends on your personal goals, and on how good your business idea is.

I had the fatal thought. I think happened to me one morning, or maybe one afternoon, during a discussion over a few glasses of wine, my thoughts drifted back to a salon owner that my wife had once worked for, she appeared to have way more than us, and seemed to work far less hours. I do remember, uttering those potentially fatal words to my wife Kylie, "We should open our own business". "Your a great hairdresser, we should be able to build a solid business".

Michael Gerber called it the E-Myth, you should read his book as well, it will help you understand systemising your services.

Cast your mind back to when you made your fatal decision. I'll bet you wanted to go into business for more than just one of the following reasons;

- you wanted to make lots of money,
- you wanted a nice lifestyle,
- you thought you deserved more for your efforts,
- you wanted to give your family a better life.

I'll also bet that you had no idea that the following would eventuate;

- You would keep your prices low in the belief you would attract more clients, so your that your clients would have more money.

- You would give most of your income to you staff,

- You would end up supporting all the other businesses in your community, the insurance companies, banks, product suppliers and the like.

Like you, Kylie and I thought we knew what we were doing. We certainly thought we knew more than our employer. We had also saved enough money to get started, or so we thought. Looking back, we actually knew very little, we probably knew less than our boss, and we certainly didn't have enough money.

Just like everyone else who opens a small business, we thought we had a great idea. Importantly, we had enthusiasm, optimism and enormous drive! We were intelligent, but naive. However we learnt very quickly. Our grand dreams for the future were very righteous. We acknowledged our moral responsibilities, gave back to the community, looked after our clients and staff, cared for our families wellbeing when we could, whilst advocating for the environment, and all the rest of the truly wonderful social aspirations.

The majority of the salon owners I have met over the years, truly believe that they must consider those aspirations and apply them to their business on a daily basis. They would never want be accused of being the most expensive salon in town, or operating like "big business," ie gouging and profiteering from the community. Never would these salon owners overcharge their clients. They may even have a business slogan or a mission statement that sounds something like, "We offer the best hairdressing at the lowest prices". They are probably really proud of the fact that they are "giving back". Unfortunately, in most cases they are giving back, before they actually get. They've got the horse before the cart! Nelly before the dray! They have everything bottom up!

Because everyone knows everything about the things they know, and absolutely nothing about everything they don't know, the do-gooders of the world, the planet savers, salon owners, frightened managers and naive hairdressers, have managed to jumble two most important goals. They cannot understand that in business there are two types of goal, personal & business goals, each containing many sub goals. Personal Goals and the goals of your Business must never cross. They are like oil and water.

Business is a Function. It's goals are matter of fact, the goals are mathematical and calculated, they are not emotional. You might get emotional, your clients could perceive your business emotionally, but the function of your business cannot be.

The Personal goals you wish to achieve can only be realised if your business reaches it mathematical target. Your personal goals are emotional, inspirational and social.

The Objective of Business is simply, to make a profit. You can give back a portion of your Profit, not a portion of your cash flow. Cash Flow is not Profit.

Enormous pressure is placed on business to do the right thing by all sorts of goodie goodies, and politically correct social groups. They too, do not understand, that to function in business you must make a profit. What you do with that profit, how you redirect that profit, is where the social rewards can be established and can be met.

There is a great Australian ethos, if you make profit, you are not operating in the community interest. Many people think that profit is a dirty word. If you use the words price, profit or money, too many times on email platforms, you will be shut down, and accused of spamming. Try to get past these naive I.T. idiots when you're selling a book about price & profit margins. I had one of them tell me that their complicated algorithms view life this way, "price = profit, profit = money making scheme, Money making scheme = spam". In Australia, a ground swell of socialism has caused the tall poppy syndrome to become rife. In general, employees don't quite grasp, that the sole purpose of business is to make a profit! And unfortunately, a majority of employees, see the cash flow, and think cash flow is profit.

When Kylie was young, she remembered her mum talking about the parents of friends that, "had money". 'They must be selling drugs to have all that money' she would say. Kylie's Mum is not alone. Many from our parents generation believe, that you couldn't become wealthy by simply working hard, investing wisely or being honest. Instead, they believe, to become rich you should be heartless, unfair or dishonest, leaving the honest hard workers of the world, destined to remain in the lower middle class. The 1920's political and unionist belief, of the evil business man, profiteering from the poor down trodden worker, is still preached 100 years on.

Many of our parents attitudes have rubbed off, and still influence many of our business discussion. We constantly have to remind ourselves that Business is the function of what we want to create. Kylie and I are eternally grateful that we have been taught to work hard. However, we have learnt to value our time and skill, to work smart and to outsource to those who specialise.We use our time to plan our business strategies. Most importantly, we are clear on how much money we need to generate to continue improving our product.

I chose to write this book in tandem with the 'Pricing Your Services' app and the'Bonus Calculation APP', in the hope I could provide Salon Owners with the tools and knowledge to make enough money to love their life. Although money alone won't make you happy, money allows choices. It's not just about a bigger house, a new car or fancy holidays, to have a choice, is to provide a lifestyle for your family, for their education and future, you can also support charity and your local community. These are the things what will make you truly happy. You could even participate in saving the planet, but only if your business makes a profit!

I have witnessed so many Hairdressers open a salon, then suddenly realise they have just bought themselves a job. A job that requires an amazing dedication to service, a job demanding long hours, lots of worry, very little help and not a leg to stand on when it comes to industrial relations. In the end you are left with no way of escape and no "good will" in the business to repay years of hard work.

In most cases, salon owners are simply passionate hairdressers who don't want to really worry about money. They just want to be passionate about their craft and enjoy hairdressing. They believe that they are the best at their profession, and that their current knowledge and education will look after them forever.

Because they have jumbled business goals and personal goals, the reality is, they've joined a world of undervalued services, simply because they don't know how to calculate a profitable price for their services. They don't want to appear greedy, don't want to be branded pushy or risk ruining their reputation, so they charge less! Thinking that a lower price is the answer to increasing their client numbers and their credibility.

I'll never understand the belief, that charging less for your time will solve your financial problems and create a stable profit. My pricing your services journey, has unveiled, some very confused owners and managers. I've had many that didn't want to calculate their Prices because, they were "scared they might have to raise their prices". I have sat down with owners and their manager only to have the manager say "this pricing thing is not for us, we have to keep our prices close to all the other salons". WHAT!!! Why don't we all stick together on deck, while the ship sinks? Correct pricing is the only way to reach any target. How does this manager know what the business needs to operate, if she doesn't know the operating costs? How does she know that what the clients are willing to pay? How did she calculate the price of a haircut? What's wrong with being the most expensive salon in town? What is her problem? May be it doesn't matter to her if the business goes under, maybe she could operate from home?

Is this "Price point fear," a problem that runs deeper than it appears? Could it be passionate stylists really want higher wages, but the prospect of charging a high price for their inexperience or having to lay their mediocre skills on the line, might really scare them, is the root cause low self esteem? Could a lack of education be the real reason for charging less? Maybe they simply don't believe in themselves.

As salon owners, Kylie & I have known the pitfalls and the successes. Our salons operated for over 21 years, during that time there were mostly highs, but also many lows, and self doubt. Upon reflection, what we needed to be successful was to be efficient with the use of our "time". The more time we took, for accurate calculation and planning, the more our self belief grew. I takes, a total mid shift to realise that, all you have is time. Time to plan, and time to sell, in fact, the only thing you are selling, is time. You need time to run the business properly, time to educate yourselves and your staff, time to mentor your team, time to coach, time to meet with the suppliers, and time to discuss growing your business. Time to grow your self esteem.

In hindsight, we should have dropped the D.I.Y. thinking, and outsourced to professionals wherever we could. The D.I.Y. mentality is the bain of the hairdressing industry. If you try and do everything yourself, all you are doing is wasting time.

Ignore Hairdressing for the moment, clear your mind and ask yourself, "What is it that I am selling?" Your clients purchase hairdressing services from you, but in reality you are selling time, a finite amount of time. The initial calculation for your prices must be based on time.Not how much product you use in each service. You provide a service that takes a certain amount of time, and your client pays for your time. There are a limited number of hours (appointments) each day, during these hours, you must make all the income you need for your business to reach its Mathematical Target. You could call this target "Seat Time" or "Appointment Time". This hourly rate is based on a cost plus a margin (gross profit) target.

All of us need to reflect and understand what our time is worth. Of course, as with all business owners the demands of operating in Australia are overwhelming, we need to be incredibly accurate.

We are threatened with fines if we make the slightest miscalculation. Government Departments generally treat Hairdressing Salons as large corporations rather than small business, operated by hairdressers with little or no business experience.

In order to escape bureaucratic harassment, you will need to keep your cash flow "positive". You must know exactly what you need, how to put a dollar figure on it, a determined time frame, and then calculate where the money will come from.

The Initial step, is to define the exact amount of money your business needs each hour, and how much each operator will need to make from each client. This amount of hourly income is your 'seat time' (appointment time). Your prices will be based on, the amount that each client will have to pay for each minute they have taken in your appointment book.

A Salon Business is about time, 'seat time'. You must comprehend the idea of potential income, and the limitations time places on how much income you and your salon can generate. You shouldn't need to be pushy when selling a service, you don't want to pressure clients to upgrade or buy unnecessary products, you only need to use a simple formula of quiet numbers, based on time. Only when your prices are too low, will you need to be pushy, and force service upgrades.

The Price that you display for your services, is extremely important. Price your time with a high value. When you undervalue what you do, your clients will undervalue your skills, as well as the services you provide. Strive to provide the very best for your Target Client Group. This could be as simple as offering comfortable rinse basins. When you can offer what your clients value, you will have found your niche.

Always have faith in what you do. Have faith in yourself and charge your worth, calculate your margins and discover how much you have to play with. Know how much income is needed for each hour of trading. Business is about securing yourself a long-term future, so you can have a fruitful life and spend quality time with your family and friends.

Schedule time to decide outcomes, be proud when your business makes a profit, set up a provision account for taxes and make weekly transfers to this account. To be successful you must decide on a specific outcome. To achieve that outcome, you need a desire to make a profit and have a formula to follow.

SETTING UP YOUR PROFIT CORE:

A business is simply "an idea", it's either a good idea or a not so good idea. If it's a good idea it will be profitable, if it's not a good idea it should be shutdown. I have many clients who have opened a second business only to find it wasn't such a good idea to try and manage both, but instead of closing one down they struggle on because they don't want to appear as failing.

Business is only an idea, it is either a good idea or a not so good idea. The primary function of your idea is to make a profit. If the income stream is less than it's expenses your idea is not so good. The only way to promote a profitable idea is to set your price correctly. There are many influences on price, but most importantly, Price must reflect the value that your clients receive. I'll get to this later, but a lower price doesn't represent greater value to most clients.

Nostri-Damus would be astounded by the crystal ball gazing abilities of the modern salon owner. Nearly every salon owner knows how much their clients are willing to pay, without doing any research, except for checking out what the salon up the road is charging. It would appear that every salon owner also has a degree in economics. Salon Owners constantly remind me that, their salon prices are interwoven with, and driven by, the laws of supply and demand, rather than reflecting the value that their clients are looking for. They also believe that these laws will force an inevitable outcome, ie lower prices.

SUPPLY AND DEMAND

"A little knowledge is a dangerous thing". I don't know who first said that, but how true. The unfortunate part is, even though salon owners, and every hairdresser, sort of understands this economic theory, they always forget the first line. ie. "**If all other factors remain equal**". No matter where I visit, salon owners and home operators always present the same observations, "too many salons", "too many home operators", "no-one puts their prices up", "I can't raise my prices because all my clients will leave" etc etc.

Because, a majority of salon owners operate, and believe, they are in a market economy. They also believe that most of their clients only shop on price. They believe this because they only know one way to price their services, ie comparison. No one has ever explained the complexities, or the methods for accurate pricing.

The laws of supply and demand <u>basically</u> state that, **if all other factors remain equal**, when we increase supply (ie more salons), service demand will decrease in each individual salon, causing the price to fall, because salon owners try to use lower price to attract more clients. On the other hand, if we had less Salons, the supply & demand theory suggests, prices would rise as salons become booked out.

In reality, the laws are a theory that will never be balanced, these theoretical laws only come into play in a noticeable form if, all other factors remain equal. By that I mean, if each salon is the same, if they all have the same skills, if they offer the same service, if they all use the same products, if their opening hours are the same, if they play the same music, if they're all in the same location, so on and so on, only if there were no variations between businesses, would the laws of supply and demand would come into play. The incorrect assumptions that are applies the the supply and demand theory are

- All things are equal *ie. Every Salon is exactly the same as yours*
- Demand is not increasing, *ie. there are no new clients entering the market*
- You cannot change market perception, *ie You cannot demonstrate to clients that you are able to satisfy their need better than your competitors.*

This is a recurring theme that will continue throughout this book. **If you can demonstrate to your clients, that you can satisfy their needs, and supply what they value, you will be able to charge top price to your market segment.**

If you are in a market price model, as most of you have placed yourself, you have become dangerously close to causing, all other factors to remain equal. In your market price model you allow clients direct comparison with your competitors. You start offering the same services and the same products, and because you continually copy each others offerings, clients find it hard to differentiate between businesses. Therefore you start to develop a supply and demand situation, you are in this market model because you assume that the salon operators around you know what they are doing.

My suggestion is to completely remove Market Place thinking from your mind and from your business promotions. If you're willing to think and act strategically, you can easily manipulate pressure caused by the supply and demand theory. You must differentiate your business and turn the focus away from price, by developing a "perceived value" mentality amongst your clients.

When you target the things that a specific client group values, you start attracting clients that are less price sensitive and are value driven. This is how you can start to move from a market price model. I suggest that each time you decide on a course of action, follow a specific procedure. It doesn't matter if you are adjusting prices, deciding on new products or services or changing the direction of your business, always follow the following procedure as a guide to business viability.

Knowledge
Accuracy
Strategy
Structure

Firstly research to gain as much **knowledge** as possible.
Secondly make sure extreme **accuracy** is used in calculations.
Thirdly decide on a **strategy** that will allow you to move
forward and improve your profit, finally set up a **structure** that
can be easily understood by your team and clients. Before
moving forward on any plan, write down these four points place
your calculations, research and plans against each of them, in
this way you will be able to clearly view your plan, you will also
be able to present your plan to others for their deliberation.

Your Salon Business can only generate a finite amount of
income. Therefore determining the limitations and potential
earning capacity that is possible within the four walls of your
salon is essential. Some obvious defining limitations, are the
number of hours you can trade, the number of workstations you
have, the number of seats in the processing area, the number of
basins, how many stylists, and assistants and how you structure
your appointment plan.

On top of that you need to determine what role you will take
within the salon. Will you act as a Receptionist / Maitre-De,
ensuring all your salon procedures are followed to maximise
your salons sales and service potential? Or will you operate as a

stylist and attempt to generate income directly from your own hairdressing skills?

You will need to place your salon pricing in a sector of the market where you can guarantee your profitability and where clients will value your services. Surveying clients to establish what they value is an ongoing, but essential management procedure, especially when new services, products and fashion enter the market.

MAINTAINING YOUR SALON PROFIT

There are three management components that are interlinked and need to be mastered by you before you can remain in control of your salon profit margin.

- Pricing your services correctly
- Customer care
- Rewards and benchmarks

There are other components that, in most cases, should be outsourced, like marketing and bookkeeping. As you work your way through this book, you will see how everything is interlinked, and hopefully you will understand how to control the components needed to maintain your salon profit.

FACTORS AFFECTING YOUR SERVICE PRICE

It's important to start at the beginning. The age-old saying, 'Poor planning leads to poor performance' is really true in relation to setting a pricing strategy.

Once you have declared your hand it is very difficult to adjust your price. Your price sends a lot of messages and is used by clients to assist them in positioning your brand in their minds.

There are **Two** clear and separate procedures to undertake before publishing the Price of your Services.

1). Calculate what you want and what your business needs. Then convert it to an hourly rate (Seat Time). This becomes the minimum price that you can set.

2). Position your business in the market by researching the services that your target demographic values and compare overall industry service price trends against your local service offering.

Deciding what you want, and calculating the minimum price to achieve this is the critical first stage. *After* you have completed this first stage, you can then manipulate your 'Seat Time' and develop market placement strategies.

All too often business owners have a pre-conceived opinion of their market placement. They enter the market without completing their calculations and before they have an accurate knowledge of their overheads, only to find they are not generating enough revenue. If your prices are too low, nothing else matters, because you won't be in business long enough to find out what happens next.

PRICING MODELS YOU MUST UNDERSTAND

There are three Pricing Models in this part of the game. The first is Market pricing, the second is Cost Plus Margin Pricing, and the third is Perceived Value Pricing. Each of these three players focuses on one particular aspect of price.

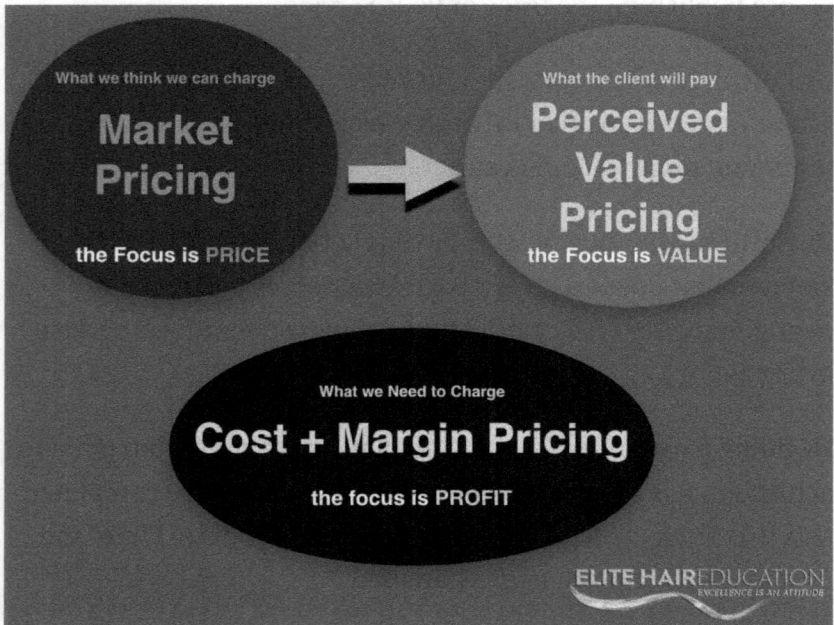

What we think we can charge

Market Pricing

the Focus is PRICE

What the client will pay

Perceived Value Pricing

the Focus is VALUE

What we Need to Charge

Cost + Margin Pricing

the focus is PROFIT

ELITE HAIREDUCATION
EXCELLENCE IS AN ATTITUDE

1). Market pricing focuses purely on Price, In this case the owner has decided that they know what each client is willing to pay, and has based this on the price that salons around them are charging, The assumption is that all the other owners around them know what they're doing. Greater than 98% of salons calculate their prices using Market Pricing as their only benchmark. Operating solely using Market Pricing will doom you to low margins.

2). **Cost+Margin Pricing focuses on Profit**, on this issue we will go into deep detail next chapter. But this is the linch pin of your business price structure. If you don't know this figure and you are unable to re-calculate it quickly you are in trouble.

3). **Perceived Value Pricing focuses on value.** This takes into account the value of your service to your clients. A Perceived Value Price reflects what a client is willing to pay. The closer you are to offering exactly what your Target Client Group values the more you can charge. This could be because you may have built up loyal clientele or offer a higher quality service or be perceived to have a higher level of skill or experience than your rivals. This is where you demonstrate your ability to deliver the service that your target market demands. This is also where you get to charge more because you can deliver.

In practice, you need to blend the three Price Models, using only a small reliance on Market Pricing. Initially you will need to accurately calculate a Cost+Margin Price and incorporate Perceived Value Pricing within the model. Only after achieving this blend do you check your position in the Market to make sure that you are not undercharging.

The most important concept to apply is 'Seat Time'. **Seat Time** is the unit of measure that you will use as the corner stone of your pricing. It is the amount your clients need to pay each minute they sit in your salon chair. Each chair will need to return $X per hour.

Your seat time is a minimum price point for your strategy. Your Seat Time is affected by the number of hours you can trade, the number of workstations you have, the number of seats in your processing area, (if you have a processing area). An example of the most underrated of all limitations is the number of basins you have. There is no point having 20 work stations if you only have two basins. Your Seat Time is also affected by the number of productive hours, downtime, wages, other expenses and dividends.

After you have calculated this initial price point, you can adjust your prices using other perceived value price methods to make sure you are charging the maximum amount that your client will pay for the value you provide.

MARKET PRICING

If you are wondering why I've chosen to start with Market Pricing, it's because I want you understand how it works then remove it from your business. In a true market price model, buyers (clients), stroll around and compare the prices of a similar product, they then make a bid, or decide to purchase based on the lowest price they can get. Salon Owners who base their prices on this model believe that all clients shop around and choose a salon only based on price. All salons offer the same service and all clients are price sensitive.

A large proportion of salon owners use market pricing to set their prices, I do mean the majority. Over 98%, more than 9 in every ten. They believe that the market price is set, and that all the other owners around them have tested this, they also believe that this set price is the highest amount that any client is willing to spend. I have no idea how a new business owner has worked that out, it's beyond me, especially when they have little management experience, and no clients survey has taken place!

But, it gets worse. The Salon Owner also assumes that the costs involved in operating competitors salons are the same as their own, then most foolishly move of all, there is no accurate calculation or projection of profit, and no consideration of value to the client, except for the inevitable offer of a cheaper Price.

The Effect of Market Pricing

Since 2008 I have been Taking Photographs of Price structures and Studying the market pricing efforts of salons in a major Shopping centre in southern Sydney. Around this time, price packaging of services was the major strength of the offer these salons were selling.

The practice continues today with good reason, price packaging or bundling is an excellent marketing ploy, provided you are in control of the offer, and you are marketing specifically to your target client, not every one that walks past. You must also make a profit from each segment of your value added offer.

Currently, the Salons at this shopping centre are opening and closing on a regular basis, and each time a new operator opens they start the same ploy of undercutting the salons around them. The graph on the next page plots their progress each year since 2008. When the price war started median priced salons were charging from $180 to $240 for a 1/2 head foils and a Cut and Blow Wave depending on the skill of the operator.

The Market Model Salons in the centre had dropped their package price to $165 and continued to reduced their prices each time a new competitor opened, until now 11 years later, the number of components in the package has increased to 1/2 head foils and a Cut and Blow Wave, and a Treatment and Make-up for $90.

Looking at the graph. The lighter shading at the top of each Column shows Profit, and the dark shading at the bottom of each column shows Costs increasing a 1.9%. You can see that profit dried up around 2015.

The background shading from $200 to $90 is the true price that the salons are charging and the line at the top is where their prices would be if they increased their prices 4% P.A. from a $165 discount starting point.

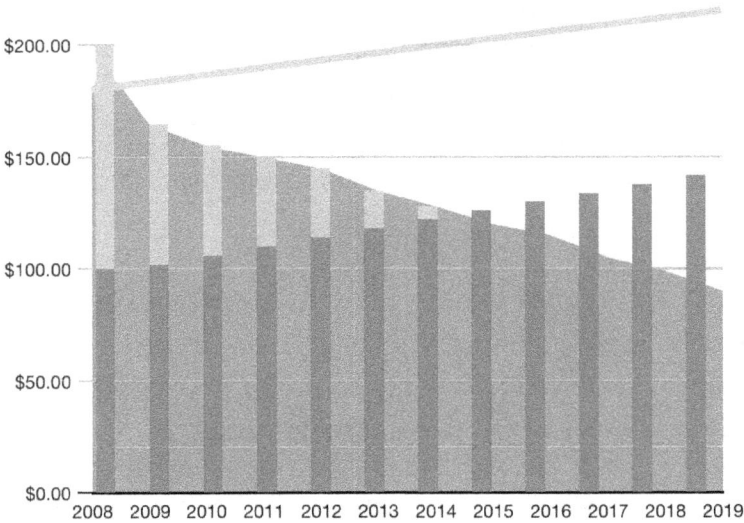

This Market Model is so entrenched it is almost impossible for these salons to change their focus from Price, to Profit and Value.

There are some shortcomings in parts of this data. Firstly the 4% P.A. price increase, is the amount I factor into my pricing, to cover expense and wage increases and CPI increases for my personal expenses. The interesting fact here, is that the Australian Bureau of Statistics says, neither the Inflation rate nor the C.P.I should be the guide for increasing prices, some industry benchmark companies suggest that prices should rise 8-10% per annum.

The second shortcoming is, that I have assumed that the salons in this price war are unable to reduce their expenses, this is reflected where I've shown profit to run out in 2015. I'm sure they have had to streamline product quality, service time, wages and rent, there would also be a need to cut the middleman on their retail and professional products. Even if they could achieve this 30% reduction in expenses, they would only be at breakeven in 2019.

Now there are group of salons appearing to operate as individuals. However, they are actually all under the same conglomerate and are controlling the prices, making it very difficult for a single owner to enter their market.

To explain a True Market Model, and what effects this model has on salon business, let's take a trip to Sydney Produce Markets and examine how the marketing model effects profit. We will also show how easy it is to start to shift the clients focus away from price towards value.

I have four photographs of apples, they all look the same. Because the market model focus is on Price, buyers initially make their choice on price alone. Even though they have a suspicion that there is something amiss with the cheapest apple.

WHICH APPLE WOULD YOU BUY ?
MARKET PRICING

69c $1.12 $1.99

Whenever I ask an audience, "which apple would you buy", the split is always very close to, 40% cheap, 40% middle and 20% high priced. I've only ever come a cropper once, when I presented this in an apple growing area of NSW, the audience could tell me all about the different types of apples I had photographed. When my only reference is price, "an apple is an apple", just as haircut is haircut. The split is the interesting point. Even though the apple were the same the "middle ground" nearly always gains the largest percentage, and the expensive apples always get around 10%, sometimes even 20% of the market.

Realising that profit margins are too low, the low price Apple growers now decide they need more than 40% of the market, their margins are so slim that it is not worthwhile continuing unless they can command as much as 60% of the sales.

Wearing their "economic genius", hats they decide to offer a 25% discount in the belief they will attract a greater share of the market. Seeing this, and without recalculating their Cost + margin needs, the other stall holders react and discount their products by 25%. This is typical market model thinking.

WHICH APPLE WOULD YOU BUY ?
MARKET PRICING

69c 52c	$1.12 84c	$1.99 $2.99 Two Apples
Special 52c this seasons Apples	Winter Special 25% off Newly Ripened Fruit	Buy Two receive 50% off your second Apple

Quite by mistake, some of them add a description to their offer. Unknowingly, they are entering the realm of "perceived value pricing".

This time, when I ask the audience "which apple would you buy", I notice subtle shifts. The shifts in preference occur because, buyers can start to do their own profit calculations and preferences. Sometimes there is a slight shift toward cheap, some time a slight shift toward expensive. This depends on where the audience sees value, although in the end the market share rarely moves by more than a few percent.

If I were to introduce a forth low price seller, the expensive apple seller would not notice any market loss, the middle price seller may loose some clients, but the low end would need to continue the price war to maintain their 40-50% of the market, until one of them goes under. Rather than entering a price war, had the Middle and High Priced Apple Growers reacted to discounting (price focusing) by focusing on value, the scenario would be very different.

WHICH APPLE WOULD YOU BUY
PERCEIVED VALUE PRICING

69c	$1.12	$1.99
"B" Grade Fruit Great Price 3-4 weeks old	Cold Storage apples 12 months old Coles & Woolies	Picked today 2am Organic,Premium Fruit Absolutely fresh

This time, when I ask an audience "which apple would you buy", using a perceived value model of pricing, something very different happens. The market share always moves towards a higher price product. Again this percentage of market share varies from region to region, because there has been many variations introduced by the seller, quality, volume, profitability. Salon Businesses, have introduced other factors like ego, vanity, freshness, health benefits, skill etc.

Which Apple would you buy? Have your thoughts changed now that a description of the value has been introduced and your focus has been turned away from price?

Even though we will discuss discounting later, lets have a quick look at the effect of the price war in this scenario

LOST PROFIT FROM A 25% DISCOUNT

85%		65%		42%
69c		$1.12		$1.99

Price of Apple	Cost per Apple	Percentage of Market	Market Price Profit	Perceived Value Profit
$0.69	$0.49	40	$1.20	$8.00
$1.12	$0.69	40	$6.00	$17.20
$1.99	$0.79	20	$14.00	$24.00

Assuming there was no change in market share and there were 100 buyers, introducing a 25% discount caused the low price seller to give away 85% of his potential profit, the middle price seller 65% and the high price seller 42% of profit.

When we moved to the Perceived Value Model all three sellers made substantially more for no extra effort.

The following example is very real and serves to show just how one can easily fall victim if you don't combine both pricing strategies and only rely on Market Pricing.

This scenario played out over a few months in a well to do suburb with a generally conservative population.

An established salon with reasonably presented decor charged of $160 for a Half head foils with a Cut & Blowdry. A new salon, with similar decor and services was opened by two ex-employees. They charged slightly under $155 in the vain belief that their lower price tactic would draw clients from their ex-employer and surrounding businesses.

A third existing salon close by, whose owner had a self esteem problem (my perception) discounted her services by 10% from $160 to $144 through fear of losing clients, even though she swore that "her staff were the best cutters in the shire". Another quite dominant matriarch actually lifted her prices from $150 to $155. Her reason? Her salon was "upmarket"! She had pink cutting chairs, and had just paid $5,000 for a leopard skin chair in the waiting area. She also told me that the salon provided her clients with "an undercover spot out the back, so they could go and have a fag". In her view this made her salon absolutely fabulous.

Finally the bottom player. The owner of a plain old salon that specialised in afro hair, he put a sign out front that gave 50% off dreadlocks on Monday and Tuesday. I don't know what he was thinking! I'd lived in the area for twenty years and had never seen anyone with an afro, and only a couple of surfie dudes with dreadlocks.

Here's the clincher, salon number 1 who charged $160 actually simply plucked his price out of the air, the best salon in the mall some five kilometres away charged $180 so he thought $160 would be a fair thing. Every Owner all the way down to the $12.50 Dreadlocks had placed their businesses in competition with a guess.

None of them knew their costs nor did any research to find out what the market could reach. Everyone of them made decisions based on price, a totally manufactured price with a fictitious basis. Worse still they all presumed that their clients only shopped on price and valued nothing else. The only one that had fluked some sort of positive, was the silly woman who had imagined her clients would pay more because she had a $5,000 waiting chair and a place to have a fag. If she had surveyed her clients, and had they perceived value from the chair, she may have been on the right track.

Cost Plus Margin Pricing

The next four sections in this chapter are dedicated to explaining how to calculate your Cost Plus Margin Target and your 'Seat Time'.

For the easiest calculation and best results, you should purchase the APP "Pricing your Services."

If you haven't, you can calculate your seat time manually using a calculator or spreadsheet, However it's handy to have the APP on your phone, it enables you to adjust wages costs and income targets quickly.

I'm honoured, and lucky enough to be allowed access to data from some of the best computer companies who providing POS software to salons operating in Australia. This helps my research greatly.

The following chart will show you the importance of accuracy in your calculation. The model for the exercise is the current median Salon in Australia. Thats all the largest salons removed and the less than two operators removed. We came up with a profitable salon model that has 4 to 5 Stylists (including the owner) and a gross weekly income of $ 11,000 to $13,000.

What Difference will a Few Dollars Make

	Seat Time Needed	$5.68 under Seat Time	+$5.68 Over Seat Time
Price that you charge	$75.68	$70.00	$81.36
Your Annual Profit	$50,000	$2	$100,073

The Chart shows that these salons needed to charge $75.68 per hour per client for their services to create a $50,000 per year profit.

If the calculations were under by $5.68 the annual profit would be reduced to just $2. Reflect for a minute on how well you know your own Cost Plus Margin Target and how much your inaccuracy might be costing you. If you relied solely on Market Pricing your prices could easily be worse than $5.68 under you Seat Time needs. You can turn your business around by simply increasing your price by a few dollars per hour

COST PLUS MARGIN PRICING.

Cost Plus Margin pricing gives you the figure you need to make a profit. It allows you to determine your minimum seat time target, from where you should develop your perceived value price.

Many economists will suggest that Cost + Margin Pricing is dead and you should go straight to Perceived Value Pricing My thoughts are, that you need a starting point and a projected income that will give you profit. For this reason Cost Plus Margin pricing should be used as the first step in building your pricing strategy and incorporated with Perceived Value Pricing.

Cost Plus Margin pricing is the standard method of pricing in business, it seeks to first determine the cost of providing a service, and then add an additional amount to represent the desired profit.

To determine cost, you need to figure out direct costs, indirect costs and fixed costs. With The Cost Plus Margin pricing approach, the thing to remember is that you have to factor in all your costs. Those costs include wages rent, utilities, administrative costs, and other general overhead costs and downtime. Your App will Achieve this with the input of accurate data.

Your Formula:

Wages (including owners) + 10% GST

Less

Cost of Retail

Plus

Dividends and Drawings

Plus

All other Relevant Expenses

Plus

Salon Profit Required

Divided by

Total Productive Hours

= Hourly Staff Target

add cost of

Downtime %

Equals
Hourly Seat Time

WAGES INCLUDING OWNERS WAGES

The first piece of information you need to collect are your Staff Wages Costs. Wages include all wages paid to staff that are shown on a group certificate or shown on your accountants report or Profit & Loss Statement for the year end.

Only add bonuses, commissions, cash payments or other payments paid to part-time or casual staff, if your accountant has included them with wages and salaries on his report.

Also, add in the amount reported to your book keeper or accountant that you record as a wage.

Make sure Superannuation and Workers Compensation insurance is in this Figure. On your P&L statement it could be separate

Wages is the only expense category on which you don't pay GST or VAT. This means to pay a wage of $100K you must generate $110K. For this reason an additional 10% of wages will be automatically added to annual income total by your APP if you are using a spreadsheet. Remember to add it to the total wages. GST is included in your other expenses categories.

RETAIL STOCK ONLY

Retail Stock only, not professional stock: (colours, basin stock etc). We will be removing the cost of retail stock from your expenses. We are calculating the cost of your service. Selling retail is not part of your service cost. Retailing plays an important part of your salon income but it should be self funding. Retailing should be treated as an independent and measurable part of your business, but it should not be included in this calculation as it is not part of your service expenses. If you cannot separate your Retail Stock using your suppliers invoices, try your computer retail sales records and use an estimate of two thirds or half of your Gross retail income depending on your mark-up. This will give an amount reasonably close to your retail cost. The higher your retails sales are, the more important it is to separate this expense.

If you are operating a Beauty Salon retail will play an even greater role a profitable beauty salon will need their gross retail sales to be approximately 50% of their gross income. The App has a calculation that allows you to add back retail profit to help lower the service price, so you will need to still remove the cost of retail for the moment.

DIVIDENDS, DRAWINGS & PROVISION FOR BONUS

On a weekly, or even a daily basis, you will be taking cash from your business for various purposes. We will call these 'dividends' rather than 'taking cash from the till.' You will also transfer, withdraw or spend money from your business account that is not a legitimate business expense and is not recorded as petty cash. These transfers are described as 'drawings,' These drawings are not recorded as personal income and not shown on your annual tax return.

'Dividends and Drawings' are not part of the salon owner's Wages or Salary. Quite often, these transactions will not appear on your group certificate for taxation purposes and need to be added to the amount of income that your salon needs to generate. These transactions are not profit either.

In this section, you should also add the amount of income you will set aside for Bonus and incentives This will give you a buffer in each weeks target to absorb some of your bonus payments. This amount could be as little as $100 per week ($5000 pa). Some of my clients allow $1 or $2 for each productive hour that they have in their formula, this amount seems to be more than enough and only raises the seat time by $1 or $2 per hour.

ALL OTHER EXPENSES:

On your Accountants report or Profit & Loss statement , all of the remaining expenses that will be relevant in the next year should be added. Check the relevancy of these expenses especially if you have purchased furniture or have completed some renovations or repairs and these expenses will not reoccur in the next year.

ANNUAL PROFIT THAT YOU REQUIRE

The last figure you need to project is your required profit.

Profit is the amount of money that you intend to reinvest into the Business in the coming year. It is not necessarily for your personal use. It will be used for things like new equipment, increased marketing, staff education, provision for taxes, annual leave, redundancy, and anything that is not in last years expenses that you would like to increase in the coming year.

YOUR BUSINESS HEALTH CHECK

Your Business Health Check

Enter the following figures from last years Accounts

GROSS Operating Expenses	Fill your Annual Expenses Below in the green cells	Target %	Actual %
Wages including Owners Wages	$150,000	40	34%
Retail Stock Only	$30,000	10	7%
Owners Dividends and Drawings	$50,000	5	11%
All other Expenses	$150,000	35	34%
TOTAL EXPENSES	$380,000	90	85%
ANNUAL PROFIT that you require	$50,000	10	11%
Required Annual Income GST Adjusted	$445,000		

On page one of your App 'Your Business Health Check'. You need five separate pieces of data, enter them into the light grey information cells shown above. Green cells on your APP.

Take note that we have included your wage and the Annual Profit that you would like to make. This means, the required annual income on the bottom line, is your target income for the year, not a just total of your expenses. The figures in the example used on this page, are for demonstration purpose only and do not represent any specific salon. However the Target Percentages are a true average salon data. If your salon operates a few percentage points either side of the targets%, your business would have strength.

Target %:

The figures in the Target % column are a guide line for a successful salon operation. These percentages are close to the Taxation departments guidelines for a hair salon although the ATO's published range is 21% to 44% of gross income (p.175). This figure in most cases does not include the full owners wage. For the purpose of setting our prices we must include the owners full wage. A very important statistic for your operation is the figure for, 'Wages Including Owners Wages', our target is 40% of your target income, a very different figure from the ATO benchmarks. It is extremely difficult to operate a salon at 40% of Target income, especially if your price structure keeps your income close to Cost+ Margin. However it is imperative that you keep your Wages expenses as close to this target as possible, preferably under the target. The simplest way to reduce your cost percentage is to generate more income, ie raise your prices.

Actual %

The Actual % column amounts will fluctuate as you adjust each of the five required pieces of information on this page. Using this percentage you can actually make adjustments to your budget so that you can operate your business efficiently. Further on in the APP as you nominate a seat time higher or lower than your needs, your profit will be adjusted. You are able come back to this page and enter your new profit amount and re-adjust your budget.

PRODUCTIVE HOURS:

Productive Hours

Calculate the Total number of productive hours worked in your salon each week
Productive Hours are hours paid where an employee physically produces income

Stylists on the Floor	Fill your Total Hours Below in the green cells
Salon Owner Hours	35
All Stylists Hours	60
2nd & 3rd Yr Apprentice Hours	72
First year apprentice on Floor	10
Total Productive Hours	**177**

In this exercise we are trying to establish <u>Potential</u> Productive Hours. We want the total of the potential money making hours that your team members are available to generate income. Not the hours marked out for meetings and manning the reception.

The hours your team is in the appointment book to take clients bookings are classed as Productive Hours

Also all the productive hours that you as Salon Owner work on the floor doing clients. As a Salon owner and Business Manager you should account for the time you spend on the floor directly generating income. Even if you only do clients for five hours a week, you should record those five hours as productive working hours. To set your service price accurately, it is imperative that all productive hours are accurately recorded.

When you setup your calculations a good idea is to breakdown the hours worked into stylist categories this will help you double check the hours that you have allotted for each team member.

Salon Owner Hours: Total all the hours that you are in the Appointment book not at reception or meeting with sales reps.

All Stylist Hours: Total every hour that your stylists are in the appointment book.

2nd and 3rd year Apprentice Hours: Total every hour in the Appointment book doing Clients (Not working as a colourist).

First year apprentice on the Floor: Only add these hours when the apprentice is in the appointment book to do clients. More than likely, this will start to occur late in their first year.

Adjusting for Downtime

The only way to calculate downtime is to count the empty time in each employees column, some Computer programs have this capability.
Most Owners and Managers tell me that their downtime is about 5% however when I've studied their appointment books the story is very different, if your overall downtime is less than 30% redo it, look for extended appointment time for running late and end of day appointments!!

Productive Hours	177
Enter the Average Downtime Hours per week in the Green cell	55
Downtime Percentage	31%

Downtime, is the most important item in your calculation. Most Owners and Managers are not convinced of it's importance, or even monitor this statistic. Even a 5% fluctuation has an enormous effect on your annual profit. If your Down time is 25% and you don't add it back, you are discounting every service by 25%

Consistent vigilance is required with regard to downtime, 'study and report, don't justify anything', there is no room for ego here. If your business is in shape, and you have a good rebooking system you should expect to rebook between 60%

and 80% of your clients. Given that, your overall downtime will be between 20% and 35%.

If your <u>overall</u> salon downtime is less than 20%, redo your calculations. All of the following items need to be classified as downtime. Catch up time, Redone services, checking that the last client of the day or shift actually turned up & making sure that the 45 minute Haircut isn't marked out for an hour. Second and Third year apprentices blowdrying, rinsing clients and applying another stylists colour will be downtime if their name has been marked out of the appointment.

If you have recalculated your downtime and the overall figure is still under 25%, increase your prices tomorrow, pat your team on the back, monitor whatever you're doing, and whatever you do, don't change your culture.

ALLOCATING YOUR SEAT TIME

Pricing Structure Summary

Your Allocated Seat Time

60 Minute Service	**$67.10**
30 Minute Service	$33.55
45 Minute Service	$50.33
120 Minute Service	$134.20
Your Staff Hourly Target	$51.19
A 38 Hour Staff Member will need to Generate	$1,945
Your Weekly Income Target	$11,877

Elite Hair Education

CONGRATULATIONS!

You have taken the first steps in controlling your business.Not many owners in your industry have actually calculated their exact needs.

You now know the minimum amount you need to charge to generate the income you wish to earn.

From here, you need to research the Perceived Value of your services, to determine if you can increase your prices or need to add more value to your product.

If you need to charge more but feel you can't, you will need to reduce your seat time by reducing your expenses or dividends or decreasing your downtime.

To improve your profit margin further, you can start to increase your prices by putting a figure on the perceived value within your current service. Keep in mind, if you charge the seat time rate that you have just calculated you will be in a position to keep your business moving forward profitably.

Your Allocated Seat Time

The prices that are shown on this page of your APP represent the minimum hourly price you need to charge for each seat operating in your salon.

I have expanded your seat time target over the first four lines on this page to give you a break down of One hour, then 30 minutes, 45 minutes and finally, two hours.

Put Simply, if you book out 30 minutes for a Haircut, you will need to charge your client, in this case $33.55 ($34). If your client is sitting in your seat for Two hours then the Price is $134.20 ($135).

The important thing to realise is, this figure is dependent on the other cost factors that you currently have in place in the salon, i.e. downtime, staff levels, associated costs etc. These have been included in your seat time calculation. Each time there is a significant change in the associated costs, you will need to adjust the specific data, allowing your new seat time rate to be calculated. You will also need to monitor your salon down time on a monthly basis and adjust this figure regularly.

If you do this you will have total and instant reporting on your salon profitability and able to plan strategies for maintaining your profit levels.

HOURLY TARGETS FOR YOUR STAFF

You will have correctly noticed on page 4 line 5 of your APP that your staff hourly target is different to your hourly seat time. This is because your staff are employed for a specific number of hours each week. There is no downtime cost attached to their target.

For example, If a staff member was employed for ten hours and staff hourly target was $70 per hour they would need to generate $700. Because they average 30% down time, the employee would normally only generate $490. If we increased our prices to $100 per hour to compensate for the average 30% downtime, your staff member would generate $700 which is in line with your staff hourly target and your seat time requirements. In this instance, each of your 38 hour staff would need to generate $2,660 per week. Do not forget, Retail Sales Income is not included in these Targets. This is a service target only. Bear in mind, this is an example, not a real case scenario.

Increasing or Reducing your seat time

Increasing or Reducing your Seat Time

Reducing or increasing your seat time by even $2 either way could have $50,000 effect on your Profit and dividends. If you believe that you can increase your hourly prices due to market prices or client perception type the rate in the green cell and your profit and dividends will be adjusted based on your input data.

Price per hour needed	$68.00
Enter the price you believe you can charge	$75.00
Your Annual Profit will now be	$114,040
Your annual Dividends and Drawings can Now be	$50,000

If you have purchased the APP, you will have this page available to help you adjust your budget. In the light grey Cell on this page you can enter the price that you believe you can charge or the price that you currently charge. Your app will automatically adjust your Annual Profit amount and your drawings where applicable. From here, you are able to go back to your salon health check on page 2 and adjust your budget until you have the balance you need to run a profitable salon.

STAFF LEVELS & STAFF TARGETS

All of us know how critical having the correct staff level is to the profitability of our business. Calculating the staff level for a salon is multi faceted. As a manager or owner you need to consider a multitude of options.

How many staff will be working at different phases of the week. Also, what skill level do these staff members need to be at?

What supervision or support do these staff members need?

Who will answer the phone and care for clients walking in for an appointment or provide advice or process retail sales?

When first addressing a staffing situation, my initial thought is 'Flexibility Wins Wars'. When planning my staff levels, I first look at the skill level of my staff, particularly those waiting in the wings ie, my apprentices and 1st year qualified stylists.

I meticulously plot their education. The quicker I can help them develop the skills to get on the floor, the more flexibility I have with my workforce.

Obviously, some times during the week are busier than others and the team needs to be spread a bit thinner than during the busiest periods. If I understand the downtime patterns within my business, and I have calculated the salon downtime accurately, the hourly income needed in the quieter times will be compensated by the adjustment for downtime in my 'seat time' calculation. I can now confidently set my staff targets.

If my Pricing is correct my team will be able to reach the income targets and generate a profit, If I have under priced my services, my team will never reach the salon needs.

You will often hear a wages target of 40% of gross income as the benchmark for staff levels. Only use this as a guide and don't let it rule your decisions. On the other hand don't let it get out of control.

Effects of Reducing Staff Hours

This Calculation on your APP will help you decide if you think you are over or under staffed as well as the effects of altering Staff hours.

Data put into the light grey cells will show you the effect on your Seat Time if you were to reduce staff hours. It can also be used to determine if you are making a profit during the hours you are considering a reduction.

EFFECTS OF REDUCING STAFF HOURS

Current Hourly Seat Time	$67
Weekly number of Staff Hours to be Reduced	38
Gross Pay for Staff for these hours (including super)	$950
Actual Average Weekly Downtime for These hours	20
Actual Average Weekly Income for These hours	$1,170
Under or Over Seat Time Target during these hours	-$775
New Required Seat Time for your Prices	$72

The First Row shows your current Seat Time requirements. In the First light grey cell, you can enter the hours you wish to reduce, or the total hours of one staff member in this example I want to reduce 38 hours.

You will then need to calculate the wages that you pay for these hours. In this example the wages are $950 for the 38 hour I want to reduce.

Next, and most importantly you need to enter the downtime that is occurring during that time period. If you are reducing a small number of hours (10-15), the downtime will probably be very high, much higher than your normal weekly Downtime Percentage.

Finally, you need to enter the average weekly income that is generated during this period. The results will indicate to you how much Profit or Loss you are making each week during this period. This is Profit in relation to your seat time targets in this case you are losing $775 over the 38 hour period.

You will also be shown the new seat time that you will have to charge if you make these changes. Sometimes, the changes will increase your seat time. This is because you have less staff to cover all costs. In this situation it is important that you juggle your reduced hours and look for ways to cut costs as well. You will find a way. Using this too, you can make very accurate decisions.

YOUR WEEKLY SERVICE TARGET

Weekly **Service** Target

In the Green Cell enter the weekly hours for individual
staff to calculate individual weekly service targets.
Remember this is a SERVICE Target.
Retails sales are NOT included in this Target.

Number of Productive Hours Worked each Week (In appointment Book)	35
Current Hourly Staff Target	$51.19
Weekly Target for this Staff	$1,792

Page eight of your APP will set your Staff Targets, based on the seat time you have calculated and the number of hours that each staff member is employed. Remember this is a services target. Retails Sales must not be included in this target. If you want to give a retail bonus, keep it separate from this target.

Please don't fall into the trap of giving a bonus or commission when they reach this target. The Bonus or Commission can only be a percentage of the amount they generate above this target.

You could choose a higher target for your team. As a bonus when the higher target is reached, you might consider paying them a percentage of the difference between the minimum weekly salon target and the actual weekly income.

To calculate each team members minimum target simply enter the number of hours paid for each individual, in the example below 35 hours has been entered in the light grey cell. The APP is showing the current Staff Hourly Target and the Weekly Target for this Staff Member $1792.

Remember, the hourly Staff Target is <u>different</u> to your seat time target.

PERCEIVED VALUE PRICING

Know Who They Are

ONE SIZE DOES NOT FIT ALL

Know What They Want

COST PLUS MARGIN PRICING V'S PERCEIVED VALUE PRICING

We have just learnt to calculate the Cost plus margin price for our services and why using Market Pricing is a deadly game.

The next concept that we must fully embrace is Perceived Value Pricing. Some believe that this is the only method that needs to be used. My point of view is that accuracy is your defence line, Perceived Value Pricing is your attack. I love a strong attack but I also need to have the support of a powerful defence to launch from.

There are some shortcomings if you use Cost+Margin Pricing as a stand alone Method. That is why we use Perceived Value Pricing in Conjunction.

The aim of Cost Plus Margin pricing is to mathematically calculate your price point, by working out your total costs, then adding an amount, which is your profit. That's what your APP has just done.

Cost Plus Margin Pricing doesn't take into consideration the amount clients are willing to pay. If you use Cost Plus Margin Pricing as a stand alone strategy, and your client derives considerable value from what you offer, your client will love you. However you could be making more profit and using that to re-invest into your business.

Cost Plus Margin pricing ignores your image and market positioning. Costs disguised as downtime, are easily forgotten or overlooked, so your true profit per sale is often lower than you realise.

Many salons have an actual average service income of 10% or more. Under the advertised price, this is due to discounting and other forms of undercharging. Cost plus Margin Pricing is designed to ensure you don't charge below your breakeven point.

The aim of Perceived value pricing, is to shift the focus from price or profit, to questions of value. Perceived Value pricing is the most highly recommended pricing technique by consultants and academics. Perceived Value pricing is an unstable concept to use as a stand alone strategy for Small businesses selling services in a saturated market. The perception of value in your service changes as your competition adjusts to your offer.

It costs you a certain amount to provide and sell a service to make a profit. But, if clients don't value what you offer, then your price will always be too high.

You will read that cost plus margin pricing is dead or that it doesn't work. The main reason that some economists state this is because using this method alone could cause you to under charge for your services, or, if you take too much profit or dividend, you could over charge for your services. This is a valid observation.

Apart from being able to charge a higher price, Perceived value pricing has Two aspects or perspectives that are prevalent in service industries, **1). finding your place** in the market and 2). charging a higher price for, **Additional Value in your Service.** It is about discovering who your target market is and what they want. When you have done this, you can charge at a higher rate because you will providing the service that your clients value.

This sounds pretty simple, but in reality focusing on the correct market requires a fair deal of investigation. The most important thing to remember it is one size does not fit all, by that I mean you cannot attract everyone that walks past your door.

I hope the following <u>true</u> story will demonstrate to you how incredibly important finding your correct place in the market really is.

For about 40 years, Joe the barber has owned his salon in the Central West of New South Wales. His personal experience is 45 years in the hairdressing industry. His routine, the same every morning. Joe would open his shop at 9:00 am, put on is perfectly pressed light blue tunic, grab his plastic chair, sit out the front of his store, read the form guide and have a cigarette. Throughout the day he would get a few customers and more than likely they would talk about the races. Saturday morning was particularly busy. All the local men would line up with their young boys to have one of Joe's $15 haircuts

Then it happened, one day without warning directly opposite his salon, a brand-new barbershop!! Owned by three young groovy guys, with groovy haircuts. Their salon looked like a teenage boys bedroom. Stuck all over the walls, it had signed football jumpers and pages ripped out of car magazines.

I noticed there were no photographs of topless bikini girls. There would've been in Joe's early days. These guys obviously ran a politically correct, new age guy type salon. Nothing in their salon was really organised. Except for a large CASH ONLY sign, the salon was pretty much a very cool mess.

The Price of a haircut at their salon started from $27.50. The only routine in their heavily booked day was to go to the bank and collect coins for the next days trading.

Joe wasn't going to take this lying down. Almost over night he had brain wave (snap), without doing any research or market testing, he decided he was going to expand the range of clients that he could attract to his salon. He decided to take a risk. Everyone knows that the price of a men's haircut at the barber is $15 and despite knowing "his" clients would not pay more, Joe bravely entered new territory he pushed his men's haircut price to $18, and with a ground breaking stroke of genius he introduced ladies haircuts at $25, in a barber shop? But wait, he could entice the ladies to bring their kids, by only charging $5 per child. $3 less than his current price! That way on Saturday when the men can in with their boys they would still be paying the same as they are now.

His extensive marketing campaign consisted of a chalk board out the front of his salon with his new prices and services written in bold white chalk. He then sat on his stool next to the front door in his freshly pressed light blue barbers tunic, form guide at the ready, and his fag hanging out of his mouth. He waited patiently for the flood of new clients to arrive.

He knew he was on a winner, after all he was a very talented stylist, he could do every haircut known to man, he also now had the cheapest ladies haircut prices in town, his salon was immaculate with beautiful vinyl flooring, three art deco waiting chairs, three real 1920's barbers chairs, no wash basin and the subtle waft of stale cigarette in the air. On the wall he had a really cool clock, a useless clock in reality, it had no numbers, just hands, anyone under 25 years old couldn't read his clock. Everything in the new world is digital.

At 9:10am, on a wet Monday morning I arrived at the groovy guys salon, I was sure I would get and appointment. Man was I wrong! When I got to the door the three "barbers" were flat out. The six waiting chairs were full. One of them shouted across the room "hey buddy come back in 40 minutes"! At this point I was a bit peeved, I felt like running across the road to the immensely talented and unbelievably experienced Joe the Barber, still sitting there in his blue tunic with form guide and fag at the ready, he was like a leopard, unseen in the background, waiting to strike. But no, I decided to wait, I really wanted a cool haircut, not simple short back and sides. For just $9.50 more, I could look like I should be on the cover of Vogue magazine! Okay, maybe not Vogue magazine, possibly senior's weekly, but I definitely did not want to look like the local cow cockie.

40 minutes past and I finally advanced to the waiting area. It won't be long now and as I waited, I listened to one of the three "barbers" tell his client that he was about to started his barbering course at TAFE next week. I'm thinking, what have I got myself into!

After a moment of panic, I thought to myself, I hope I don't get him, but this kid looks like he know's what he's doing, his hair looks good, and he's dressed for the part, he is also working at the teenage boys bedroom. Wait a minute! These guys have actually sold this to me, I'm thinking like the clients they are marketing to, not like an Intelligent 60 year old man.

Finally, I got my haircut, it wasn't exactly what I asked for, actually, it wasn't anything like what I asked for, but I looked great, I could've been on cover of Vogue, cool haircut, fitted suit, I felt good, and it only cost me $27.50. I'd just paid that for breakfast.

All the while I was checking out Joe the barber across the road, he did not have one client, yet his salon was immaculate and his prices were 30% lower than the teenage boy's bedroom. Joe the barber had 45 years more cutting experience, he could give me any haircut I asked for. My pet hate is waiting, had I gone to Joe I would have been finished an hour earlier. Why wouldn't I go there?

Joe's extensive marketing campaign hadn't attracted a single new client. The problem was, no one knew what his business stood for, except, cheap price haircuts. The image he portrayed in his freshly pressed blue tunic, form guide and fag, shouted only one thing "short back and sides".

Even though Joe was a very talented stylist he hasn't demonstrated that to me, or any other potential client. As for a saving of $9.50, who would take the risk?

Joe certainly had not attracted any female clients. No Fashion conscious female would go to "Joe the barbers". Not at any price. He wasn't going to get any children during school hours either, except for the sick ones. I think his marketing campaign had seriously missed its mark.

After, my haircut, I sat in the coffee shop next door and watched Joe the barber. During the next few hours he only had one client, a bloke that looked a bit like "Horrie Jumbuck". He must have just come in from the paddock. I guess they talked about the form guide, and the three dollar price hike Joe had imposed on his haircut clients, maybe they just talk about the time. I didn't actually see what Horrie's hair looked like. As he walked out of the barbershop Horrie pulled his Akubra tightly down over his head hiding every inch of Joes creative hairstyling.

What has the experienced, Joe the barber done wrong?

Why were the inexperienced "barbers" at the teenage boy's bedroom fully booked?

Joe the barber's presumption, that everyone in town only purchased on price was a terrible mistake. When he Pushed his men's haircut price up a little because the salon across the road was charging nearly $30, he made his first intelligent decision. He should have put his prices up eight years earlier.

Joe should have asked Horrie, and clients like him what they value, then incorporate those ideas into his business. The focus being on the needs of his clients and what his clients value. Joe's advertising needed to push value, not price, for starters Joe should be promoting his 45 years experience.

To develop his new business plan Joe's first step would be to calculate his cost plus margin price then add value based services to his business. If Joe had been armed with financial knowledge and some new value offerings, he hopefully would be able to move his price equivalent to, or higher than others around him.

Joe's problem was, that he's trying to attract everyone on the street, the most common mistake salon owners make in their marketing decisions. If after making these changes, Joe decided to change his business model and attract female clients. His next step would be to survey potential female clients to find out what he needed to do to attract them. More than likely, he would need to change the business name, dress up his salon, and definitely changed his personal image, that means no more blue Barbers tunic, he may even need to throw out the form guide and provide more suitable reading material. Most importantly Joe would need to find a way to demonstrate, that he could provide his existing and potential clients with the service they wanted and valued.

It's very obvious that Joe the Barber understands that he needs more income. It is also obvious that he has not calculated the costs of operating his business, nor the profit he wishes to take. I would imagine the actions he would take to improve his business would be vastly different if he had an accurate handle on his bottom line.

Joe's Business management style is called "flying blind." It's case of only knowing what you know, and knowing nothing about everything you don't know.

Joe has no understanding of his market or how to place his business correctly, he has no knowledge of perceived value pricing or the cost plus margin model, he doesn't even know these things exist. Joe has been in business for a long time. Most likely he's just keeping his head above water, and now, as more sophisticated younger operators move in, Joe's business will probably just fade away.

The Teenage boys bedroom on the other hand, also invented their price structure. Through sheer luck, or maybe by a simple uneducated guess they placed their prices slightly under the average female haircut in the region. They have a reasonable understanding of their market. They've realised that men want to look well groomed, and fashionable. $27.50 is really inexpensive, maybe even too low. When you take a deeper look at their prices, even if they worked at full capacity with no downtime all day, and no breaks, these guys are looking at around $80 an hour gross income, Beard Trims, Shaves, lunch and toilet breaks would reduce this even more, unfortunately after all the other expenses in running a business this only gives them a take home of about $50 an hour.

It gets worse! I'm sure there is a downtime period in this business, and of course there's no holiday pay or sick pay when you work for yourself. After all is factored in, the reality is these guys are working really hard and they'd be lucky actually earn more than $40 an hour.

"The teenage boys bedroom" guys have done a wonderful job of placing themselves correctly in the market, I wonder if their price structure would be different, if they used a cost plus margin pricing model, in conjunction with perceived value pricing to set their price structure, rather than using competitive or neutral pricing models in conjunction with their uneducated guess.

A short Post script to Joe's story. I drove through the town recently only to find Joe's business closed. It has been replaced by a Salon specialising in Ladies Cut & Colour. Beautifully decked out and appearing reasonably busy.

Joe appears to have been pushed out of business by a salon charging, <u>double</u> his price.

So much for the industry held belief, "if I raise my prices all my clients will leave". The fact is, whoever delivered what the clients valued, stayed in business. Price had nothing to do with this outcome.

FINDING YOUR PLACE IN THE MARKET

Without delving too far into the world of marketing, you do need to be able to answer the following questions in order to establish who to target, and to determine if you are on the right track.

- Who Am I Targeting?

- Why Have I Chosen This Demographic?

- What Does This Group Value?

- Am I Capable Of Providing This Groups Values?
-
- Can I Demonstrate This ?

Have listed some of the things that clients in certain groups might value. This will help you to start your list. There are many more things you could add and things that you could remove. Your list will need to be very specific to the group that you choose to target.

Opening Times	Vanity
Service Time	Pride
Convenience	Peer Pressure
Family Needs	Self Esteem
Previous Experience	Skill
Happy Team	Reputation
Fun Uplifting	Fashion Savvy
Ambience	Additional Benefits
Ego	Added Value

How Do you Identify the right Client?

Every clients is different, just as all business are different.

Which client do you think about when doing this analysis?

You firstly must create a list of common traits, remembering that there could be a wide variation from the expected result. This is why you are doing this exercise.

You are trying to find your market. You cannot and should not try to attract everyone who walks past your front door.

Don't skip this step. Even if it gives you the same client demographic and price range you are currently using, it forces you to think about your client's decision-making process. This is valuable to you.

We've listed some categories that will help you get started. Your list could contain many more or just some of these.

You will be able to gain most of these answers from your salon's computer data.

Age Group: The majority of your clients will come from an age group within a 15 year span, ie 18-30yrs or 25-40yrs

Post Code: Over 90% will be from your post code or adjacent. Surprisingly few will travel.

The Size and Age of their Family: This is a hard one, but your information could be dramatically altered by this statistic, particularly if your core group is 25-40 years old. A client in this group whose disposable income may be restricted financially due to the size of a young family, doesn't necessarily compromise on their grooming or appearance. Where they shop and where they eat may or may not be in line with your service offerings.

Where they Shop: The type of store that the majority of your clients purchase from will tell a lot about their standards and how much disposable income they have. i.e. David Jones v's Best and Less

- What Restaurants do they go to?
- What Music do they Listen to?
- What Magazines do they Read?
- What is the most popular service these clients buy from you?

After you have completed a survey of your main client demography, choose some clients who purchased from you and do this analysis. Then find some clients who don't buy from you and do this analysis again.

The Clients who buy from you and those who don't, value your service differently. As a marketer, your target market should be the clients who value your advantages. Hence, you should price for those clients.

For your business, the important thing to ask your clients is, who they would buy from and what would they have bought, if not your product or service? Their answers tell you who your toughest competition is.

This still does not give you the 'right' answer. It only gets you close. You can now see how your clients are making decisions and you have created a calculated price so you can see if it makes sense. Eventually, you have to tweak this price up or down based on your Seat Time, judgment and experience.

In general, if a salon owner is trying to reach a broader market, they will be tempted to reduce their price. However, a better strategy may be price segmentation. In addition to determining your Service Seat Time, you have to determine whether you will charge all your clients the same amount or whether you want variable pricing. Some salons charge more for staff members with greater expertise, they charge seat time plus an additional margin.

This could be a way to pay a commission to your staff without altering the seat time balance. In general, think carefully about charging different prices to different clients. This often will create 'ill will'. Make sure that the price structure is well documented and easily understood by your staff and clients. A business cannot afford to lose is its integrity and respect among clients.

You should always be testing new prices, new offers, and new combinations of benefits and premiums to help you sell more of your services. Raise the price and offer a bonus or special service for the client. Measure the increase or decrease in the volume of the services you sell and the total gross profit dollars you generate.

Pinpointing Your Place in the Market

When you consider your price strategy, it's important to think more broadly than simply "price." Before you decide on your pricing strategy, a final discussion on the following questions may help you to pin point your pricing.

- Are you creating a new sector?

- Who is your target audience?

- Who do your target audience currently use or who might they compare your service with?

- What advantages or benefits do you offer? Do clients value those advantages and see them as worthy of changing to your salon for their service?

- Who are the competitors?

- What price do they charge?

- What differences do you offer in comparison with the competition?

- Is the market growing or is it a well-established static market?

- Is purchase likely to be repeat or a one off? e.g. Weddings.

- What risk are clients taking in choosing your product or service? (Should they be offered guarantees or reassurances?)

By answering these questions, it is possible to get a better understanding of where your services fit into the market.

.

WHAT IS MY MARKETING PLAN ?

After you have completed your surveys and understand what your target market values you will need to draw a mental picture of where your business sits and where your target market would like you to be. On the next table you can see that on the left side I have Value based service list for clients who don't care about price and will pay anything for what they want on the right I have the opposite. Again this list is incomplete and you will need to add as many things that you can that are relevant to your situation. The object is to Tick what your clients expect from their service, then cross what your salon is currently offer to them. Doing this exercise will help your plans to improve your focus towards your chosen Target Market.

VALUE BASED SERVICE RARELY PRICE SENSITIVE									PRICE BASED SERVICE VERY PRICE SENSITIVE
Exclusive by Appointment			✓					✗	No appointment
Will Pay for what they want		✓		✗					Won't pay for extra
High Quality Refreshments	✓				✗				no refreshments
Highly skilled &	✓		✗						Varied skill & experience
Private one on one service		✓					✗		with whoever is available
Expensive Decor		✓					✗		Basic Fit Out
Priority Booking		✓					✗		Unknown Finish Time
Open Evenings & Sunday		✓			✗				No Preference

Perceived value pricing means pricing based on the value you deliver to a client. Perceived value to the client is where a lot of the subjectivity comes in when setting a price for a service.

To shift the focus from price to questions of value, You need to be aware of what competitors are charging for similar services in the marketplace and be aware of what your clients value in the service that each business is offering. This information could come from competitor websites, facebook, phone calls, talking to friends and associates who have used a competitor's services or other published data. When you know what your competitors are including in their service, you can increase your price for each item in your service that is additional to theirs.

You should compete on demonstrable value. You shouldn't compete on price if you can avoid it. Demonstrable Value would be things like, service, ambiance, skill, higher quality, exclusivity or any other factor that sets you apart. If you compete on price to win a client, you must consider whether that client will be loyal to you if they find someone offering a service at a lower price.

Your main business objective is to establish a long-term relationship in the marketplace by providing your clients with tremendous Perceived Value in terms of service and quality.

I'll use this example to explain Perceived pricing in it's purest form, and why you can charge more if it benefits your client regardless of what the "normal Price" of your service is.

Our company solicitor had his hair cut with us regularly, when out of the blue he stopped coming. So I phoned him, the problem was the price of his haircut, $40. The Forty Dollars wasn't the real problem. Initially, he would book 30 minutes out of his diary to walk across the road to have his haircut AND he would be back in his office in 30 minutes.

For some unknown reason, perhaps simply familiarity, the girls would run late when starting and finishing his appointment. This caused him to mark out an hour every time he needed a haircut. Len's hourly client charge was $360 which meant his haircut cost him $400. He was prepared to pay $220 for a 30 minute haircut, which amounted to $180 for his time, and $40 for me. But $400 was a little steep.

My first reaction was to apologise and give him a discount on the $40 haircut, hoping to get him to return. Instead, I decided to charge him $100 and book out an hour in my appointment book. I called it a Priority Booking. Len could then arrive any time in the hour and we would start his haircut immediately. He was in the salon for 30 minutes, his haircut cost him $100, but he was in control.

The Salon now had a $100 booking, my seat time was $70 so I made more on the hourly rate and my client was happy, even though I charged him $60 more. Why? Firstly, I gave my client exactly what he wanted, I also stoked his ego with the exclusive Priority Booking. In reality he could squeeze an extra 30 minutes productivity out of his day i.e. $180. He could arrive a little late and he knew he would only be 30 minutes away from his office. Because I knew my seat time, I could ensure I didn't undersell the hourly charge.

Perceived Value Pricing depends on the strength of the benefits you can prove or demonstrate to your clients. You can then set a price you believe clients are willing to pay, based on the benefits your business offers them.

If you have clearly defined benefits which can give you an advantage over your competitors, you can charge according to the value you offer your clients. While this approach can prove very profitable, you will alienate potential clients who are driven only by price, if this is your marketing plan so be it, your profitability and can also draw in new competitors as they begin to copy your offer.

Creating a Perceived Value Price works similarly to how your clients make their decisions when they deliberate about which product to purchase.

Imagine you want to buy a can of Hair Spray. Two cans catch your eye. The store's own-label can for $16 and a branded product for $25. How do you choose? You ask yourself; is the brand name can worth $9 more?

To answer this, you think of everything that is different between the two cans. You may have had better experiences with the branded variety. One may be environmentally friendly. One may be shaped differently. One may have a prettier label.

One may contain more hairspray. It's completely up to you as to what you think is important. After you've determined the important differences, you place a value on them and then decide if the branded can is worth $9 more than the own-label can of hairspray. Of course you don't actually do these calculations. But that is how your mind makes the decision in a matter of seconds.

In order to set appropriate prices, you need to understand what your clients value. Figure out the value of your service to the client, then take a slice of that value to arrive at your price.

In order to price, based on value, you need to understand exactly what your client values and your point of differentiation to your competitors. The Value in your price point must be demonstrated. After all, it would be difficult to price your service at $300 if your competitors were pricing at $150, while both provide the same perceived value to the client.

It is extremely risky to simply base your prices on Perceived Value only. You must first know your Cost plus Margin Price.

I'll say it again. A combination of two strategies, **Cost plus Margin Pricing** and **Perceived Value Pricing** are necessary to maximise your salon profit. These strategies form the basis of your core price structure. Only by combining these two different pricing models can you develop an effective and flexible pricing model for your salon.

The Steps to combining these strategies are knowing:

- What it costs you to provide your service?

- What your competitors are charging

- How clients perceive the value of your services.

In every market there are a range of clients who value different things. When we opened our original salon we had a very popular Barber shop about five doors up from us (not Joe). His price for a Haircut ranged from $15 to $25, he was completely booked out. To get an appointment with him on a Saturday you needed to sit in a line and wait for around 45 minutes. In our Salon, the Price for a men's Haircut was $49. Each client had an appointment and arrived just before their appointment time. We were also totally booked out every Saturday.

This is a perfect example of offering clients what they value, and targeting the correct market segment.

Even though we both offered Men's Haircuts, we weren't in competition with each other. Each business offered a very different product to different clients. Neither were right or wrong or better than the other. Each business offered what their clients valued. That's why we were both booked out.

Our clients were offered a free Premium Beer. If a client had two beers it only cost us $5, some clients only had one ($2.50) some none , our clients were also given a complimentary shampoo and scalp Massage that took about 5 minutes, (no extra seat time. The clients, were also given an appointment time and we lived and died by that appointment time. We almost never ran late.

Clients could also book-in for an additional 15 minute Scalp Massage for $25, this lifted our average Men's ticket value. On Saturday it was around $57 that equates to $114 per hour or $912 income per men's stylist on Saturday.

The Barber, on the other hand, could average three clients per hour against our two. That equated to between $45 and $75 (max) per hour or between $360 and $600 income per men's stylist on Saturday. We would almost double the Barbers income generation on a Saturday and our only additional overhead for the day (beer) came to around $40.

Here is my point. The barber attracted clients who liked going to the barber, and he did an excellent job of keeping his clients happy. He attracted the market he targeted. On the other hand we attracted clients who like going to a premium salon, and we did an excellent job of keeping our clients happy, we attracted the market we targeted. Even more important was the fact that both of us knew our costs and didn't get involved in a price war. The barber owned his shop and his overheads were extremely low. His seat time was around $36 per hour per chair. He could comfortably make that even if he charged $13 for a haircut, mine seat time, on the other hand, was around $85 per hour per chair, the lowest I could cut my price to was around $45, incidentally we were both only netting $20 - $25 profit per chair, each hour, for men's haircutting. Imagine, if, like every other salon owner, I used the market pricing model in this situation. I would have started offering haircuts for $25 or less. I would have had to cut the service time, and the service content. I would have been operating at a loss, because my staff would have been continually telling me that we are the most expensive salon in the town. All the while, Joe's barber shop would have fully booked, and making a profit due his low overheads. Worst of all, I would have lost clients because my offering wasn't what they wanted. Not due to the price I charged.

SETTING VALUE-BASED PRICES

Perceived Value Pricing is about setting a price for your service to capture the value that a potential client perceives. This takes "Guts." But it is the difference between winning and losing.

Here is **one** theoretical method **proposed by an economist.**

If you can get your head around it you're pretty good, It can work if you understand your business and your business is currently well placed in the market. "Have a go" at understanding what's put forward. It is certainly worth the effort. After you have formulated your answer. I'll give an example of how to apply the idea.

1). Identify your client's "second best option". This will be the salon your client would choose if she went to another salon.

2). Determine the price point of "second best option". If this option is lower than your seat time, use your seat time as your starting price.

3). List all of the ways that your service offering is better than the 'second best option'. Estimate how much you think these differences are worth **to your clients** and add this value to your Seat Time Price

4). List all of the ways that the 'second best option' is better than yours. Be very honest here. How much do you think these are worth to your clients? For each point you cannot or do not wish to match, deduct this value from your service price.

To calculate the best price — Use the price of the second best option (in step 2) <u>plus</u> the value of your advantages (step 3) <u>minus</u> the value of the second best option's advantages (step 4).

Perceived Value Price = (Step 2 + Step 3) – Step 4

Don't attempt this after a couple of glasses of wine. It will do your head in. It does work, but it requires accuracy and a lot of thought.

The following example might help you focus your thoughts.

I have decided that I can gain a market advantage by introducing an education culture into my salon, I also understand that I'll need to demonstrate to my clients my salon's expertise. My perceived value pricing model looks like this.

My annual Education Budget for the staff will need to be $10,000 that's $200 each week. I service 100 clients each week that now equates to $2 per client to cover my education budget. However, by introducing this education culture I am meeting what my clients value. By marketing correctly, my clients will perceive that my salon has a superior education culture (i.e. current fashion, better skills). How much is this perception worth? I believe that it is worth more than the $2 cost, I should be able to charge $5, $10 or maybe $15 more than other salons in town, (the market,) provided I can demonstrate this and provided my clients perceive I am exceeding my competitors skill level?

Think about this, at $15 more I'm now making an extra $1300 per week for my $2 per client education investment. That doesn't even take into consideration the increased number of clients I should attract, the higher value services I can provide and the better quality staff that my business will attract because of the education culture.

This is where theory and courage meet. When you can clearly demonstrate that you can exceed your clients expectations you can charge more for your service . Determining "how much" more is the courageous issue.

MONITORING AND CHANGING YOUR PRICE

I've said this before. You must regularly re-evaluate your costs and profit. By regularly, we mean monthly, and every time a staff member leaves or is added. You should set a monthly date to have all your reports in and evaluated. This is a time expensive exercise, but the return is great.

You must continually monitor your downtime. A change of a few percent in downtime has a huge effect on your Seat Time Target.

Using your APP, the re-evaluation can be done quite quickly once you have entered your salon reporting data for the first time. Remember that your biggest costs are usually your staff wages and their productivity / downtime.

If you can't sell services at an acceptable profit, the problem may be that your employee costs are too high rather than the service price being too low.

Salon Owners rarely spend enough time analysing their financial statements. Generally, no one has ever shown them how. We've even met salon owners who refuse to write down their expenses. Make sure you know the amount to which every person and service item is contributing to your profit each month. You're driving a business, not operating a charity.

FOCAL POINTS OF YOUR PRICE STRATEGY

1). You must know the cost of your services. That is, the business costs, margins, selling numbers, how much would you like to earn from the business and so on. When you know these numbers, you will know exactly how much each particular service will cost you. The "Pricing your Services" APP will calculate this for you.

2). Forecasting: You must perform a forecast of your sales and expenses for the next period. This can be obtained from previous performance history with adjustments for increased prices, staff numbers and seasonality. You need to know what services & products are most profitable and those you are not selling.

3). You must perform Market Analysis. You can do this by looking at competitor costs, prices, offers and possible reactions regarding the same or similar services. If you find the same or similar services sold by your competitors, you can compare your price and then conduct an analysis of your margins. Then find ways to improve value.

4). If your competition are selling their services for a price so low that your seat time doesn't allow, you must check your business costs and find possible ways to decrease them or change to another market. Or look at bundling or service time reduction.

5). Review your selling forecast. Can you sell more services? If your competitors sell their services for low prices, and you've cut all possible costs, but you still cannot obtain their prices, you must find other ways to find ways to value add, so that you can improve your market share and increase your sales.

6). Make sure you are offering what your clients value. Pin Point your "Place" in the Market. Think about your image. If you build a prestigious image, you could increase your prices. This is one strategy that will make your services become perceived as of a higher quality than the services of your competitors.

7). Combine additional services with your current services. This will increase the value of your service to your clients.

8). Your Mission Statement, Client offering, Service Policy (or what ever you would like to call it). Make sure that you have one. Make sure your clients know what's in it and make sure you live by it.

Here is a simple example. "We promise to finish our clients on time". This has been one of the more important offers that we have made to our clients. Remember the story about our solicitor earlier in this book? From a Perceived Value Price view point,He valued our haircut at $100, provided he was given the value he sought.

The point is, our solicitor, like most of my clients, value their time. From that day onward, running on time was a priority in our business, I'm still amazed how many clients valued that single important thing. Time!

As our stylists became more aware of the importance of finishing on time, and as they found more way to always finish on time, and as they realised there were bonuses for doing so. Our policy was changed. We promised our clients, that we would finish them on time, or not charge them for their Blow-dry. Our service policy was designed to put our clients needs first. Our prices were well above the market price, but without doubt our clients were happy to pay for the privilege of always leaving the salon on time.

PRICE STRATEGY

Business is about providing and creating value.

In order to set appropriate prices, you need to understand what your clients value.

You provide a valuable service when the client can't provide it for themselves.

YOUR SALON PRICE STRATEGY & STRUCTURE

Your pricing strategy and structure is not simply a tag on your salon services. Price, is not just a number you have come up with to place on your service menu. Your Price communicates to your clients, your businesses intended value positioning and also determines your profitability, price is the only factor that will determine if you reap in profits or suffer losses.

Effective design and implementation of a pricing strategy is the corner stone for your profitability. A well Managed business will have a great deal of flexibility when it comes to setting prices.

When you purchased this book, you traded some of your Services (income from services) for some of my Services (This Book). The Value is based on the information what we provide, and what you value in return (improved profit). Money simply facilitated the transaction.

Money is a measure of value, not the face value of the cash exchanged. When I get my haircut for $60 it does not mean that haircuts have a value of $60. It simply means each party valued the exchange greater than what they provided or paid, i.e. the hairdressers time and the clients cash.

Prices are not measurements of value, price is a historical fact, indicating that in this case, at a given place and time, two parties exchanged the service of a haircut for the amount of $60. At any given point in time, or during any measurement of value, the price only needs to match the value to arrive at an agreeable price point.

Methodically pricing your services is a time consuming, critically important procedure. Unfortunately many owners simply take a guess and set by comparison. Pricing your services is far more difficult and important than pricing a product, as your service price is critical to your profit line.

Service pricing, is more subjective than product pricing. Accountants, tend to price services like products, they focus on expenses and wages committed to the service, and the cost of the product used in each service, then plonk on a margin, and voila! Here is your price. This method, ignores the many variations that you can bring to your clients experience, in your salon. You need to calculate the worth of your skill, your staff's expertise, the value of your time, and which type of client your will attempt to attract. You can however, use your accountants, pricing guidelines, to figure out your costs, operating expenses and your target profit when setting a price for services.

When you undervalue your service price, you sell your services under their real market value. By doing so you've reduced profit to your business. You may have enough clients and enough income but not the profit. The APP you have used to calculate the minimum hourly rate for your services (seat time), will help you keep your prices above the minimum you need to earn if you regularly update the data. It still doesn't avoid the error of undervaluing your service prices. You need continual market research and have a price rise strategy in place, other wise you will be leaving the cream on the table.

When you overvalue your service price, you are selling your services at prices that are well above your clients perceived value. In this situation, you could lose some clients and your income and profit will decrease. **You must comprehend the following point**, this is the corner stone of perceived value pricing. The overvaluation, isn't necessarily that the client can't afford to pay the amount of money your asking for the service, and the overvaluation isn't because the client can get the service cheaper down the road. The overvaluation is, the client believes the value in your service isn't equal to their expectation. Overvaluation is not necessarily a terrible mistake, as you now have a lot of flexibility in your marketing strategy. As with undervaluing you must have continual market research and a price adjustment strategy in place.

You must remember that you are not trying to attract every single person. You are only trying to attract clients within and close to the demographic you want to attract.

If you decide to present your business as a lolly pink, 'Miss Frilly' style salon that charges $180 for a haircut, you will not appeal to the local bricklayer, or to the client that is used to paying $30 for their Cut and Dry. Don't be offended if this demographic doesn't like your salon. They are not your market.

You should be worried if they actually do turn up! Your salon is probably in the wrong location or poorly presented. I'd suggest your marketing team re-evaluate and take another approach. You will probably find the $30 Cut & Dry client will tell everyone why they are not coming back. They won't be saying it's "because I can't afford to". They will be telling stories of poor service and poor value for money.

I would like to tell you a story about a pricing strategy to highlight how the Perceived Value of a product is often very illogical. I hope I can highlight the need to know your costs and combine them with a strategy.

Years ago we decided to bundle our services to gain a higher ticket value. We bundled together a Full Colour service with a Blowdry for one price $200, then we added $40 if the client had a Haircut with the colour service. If the client decided on the $240 total package they could also purchase one retail item for $5. On top of that, if they rebooked for the total package six weeks or less, the haircut would be free that's $40 off, if the client changed their booking they had to pay $40 for the haircut. This sounds like a crazy give away, but study the following results.

The total income for the service became $205 every six weeks, as against $290-$315 every 12 weeks. The clients perception was that we had discounted our service between $85 and $110 per client each visit. This was marketed as additional value and savings, for client loyalty, not a discount.

As a result, most colour clients began returning to the salon, every four to six weeks, instead of the usual ten to 12 weeks, the overall average worked out to be 4.5 extra visits each year, for 80% of our colour clients.

When it came to the $5 product very few clients would only buy a shampoo. They always needed a pair so they purchased a conditioner or styling product as well, our retail increased dramatically. The income from our colour business increased upward of $98,000 P.A. Even better our clients always looked great, they were always being complimented because they were returning for a cut and colour every four to six weeks and our colour client base gradually increased through recommendation.

We had absolutely honed in on our Target Market and increased our sales. Our clients perceived that they were paying less even though we had significantly increased the amount of money each client payed us annually. In reality our clients needed to justify their visit to the salon, which became, always looking good and the deal they got on their Visit. The price of the service didn't really matter so long as they got a bargain to justify their spending.

Can you see how a clients perception changes when they focus on a free haircut and a $5 product, provided they rebook (value). Plus the fact their hair would always look good (vanity / pride). Rather than placing the focus on a 20% discount (price).

The exact same strategy with a price focus would have been to offer a 20% discount on a Colour package and a 45% discount on Retail. It doesn't sound as good as a free haircut or a product for $5 saving you $75. If we had focused our marketing on percentage discounts we would have run the risk of clients sticking to their normal eight to 12 week cycle while still discounting our services.

This Perceived Value Strategy increased our income dramatically. If we had used a Percentage Discount Strategy the increase in trade would have been far less, even though they were in essence the same strategy.

The key thinking in this Strategy is to shift our clients focus from price to value. PERCEPTION IS REALITY.

THE ABILITY TO DELIVER YOUR STRATEGY

Often, you can clearly demonstrate the shift from price to value. The Education of your team, and their ability to deliver on your promises, is crucial to your business strategy. The value can clearly be seen be your clients. Believe it or not there are many salon businesses who don't have a price rise strategy and who have no education plans. Many also expect their apprentices, and stylist to pay all of their education costs. I believe, both parties benefit greatly from continual education, so both parties should contribute. Even though, the industrial laws require payment from the salon owner only.

Whether right or wrong, these industrial laws have spelt the death nell, to the education needs of many young stylists, and because apprenticeships have been reduced from 4 to sometimes 2 years, salon owners have been forced to reduce the number of apprentices they employ, Salon Owners, simply cannot pay full wages to someone, who cannot generate enough income to cover costs. As a whole, salon skill level has fallen behind, and because salons undercharge they have no money for the education of their team. Recently, a product company wanted to promote our Education programs as a collaboration between our businesses, to help improve the skills in their clients salons. We had a meeting with their agents to discuss the plan and roll out the possible advantages in partnering with each other.

Some of the agents embraced the offer and used our education as a cold calling tool, to help build their presence in certain regions. One of the agents totally dismissed our offer, her focus was on the price of our education, it was nearly double that all other educators that she had used in the past. Her claim was, "Her clients would never pay our price, we were far too expensive". My question to her was, "How do you quantify expensive?" At no stage was she interested in hearing the content or the specific outcomes we were offering, just the price.

Generic education with the little specific outcome, no matter how well it is presented, is a waste of time and money, it returns little in the way of measurable income.

Well planned education that contains specific lesson plans, tailored to individual stylists, will ultimately cost nothing because the returns are immediate and ongoing.

The formula for how expensive education is looks like this:

Cost = Return minus Price

If the return is less than price the Education is a very expensive waste of time. If the return is higher than the price the Education cost nothing. For a few hundred dollars more we were able to provide specific education that returned an immediate profit to the salon owner. In this case, no matter what the price, the education cost is nothing.

PRICELIST STRATEGY

The **Price** you charge for your services, is a compromise between what you think your service is worth, and what your clients think your service is worth. Unless there is a some indication of what the client will receive, and how much they are likely to pay, you will lose many potential clients.

I am always surprised at the number of salons, that <u>don't,</u> display a PRICELIST for their potential clients. Your pricelist is the window to your business, clients are very reluctant to enter a salon unless they have fairly good idea of what they are going to have to pay.

I've heard some classic excuses for not having a pricelist, Here are some of the beauties, "It's too hard to write our prices down

because we can't quote colour without seeing the client".
"Clients will be able to compare our price to other salons,"
"Printing a Pricelist is no good because, we <u>might</u> have a price
rise". "If I print a price list my competitors will know my prices"

And finally, my all time favourite, "We don't need a pricelist
because our salon is in an arcade, and all our customers are
from word of mouth, so they already know our prices".

When I heard that one I nearly passed out, of course your
customers are word of mouth, no one knows you exist. Imagine
if you had an A-frame on the street, on it you could have a
condensed pricelist, with a map, and your opening hours, and
the product brands you recommend, and the expertise you
have, and maybe even a photograph of your decor, or your
team. You could have your contact details and social media
information on the pricelist as well. You pricelist, is just sitting
there, 24/7 waiting for potential clients. All of that information
goes on your pricelist, it's not just a pricelist, it's a tool to help
your clients <u>choose you</u>. They also get to show their friends. If
you have a pricelist you might need to put on more staff, you
might need to put your prices even higher. Wouldn't business
be wonderful if everyone knew where your business is, when it
was open, and what value you provided. Wouldn't business be
wonderful if only 10% of your clients came from word of mouth.
You would be so busy, you wouldn't be able fit any more clients.

THESE ARE THE RULES FOR A PRICELIST:

- *Concise and Easy to Understand:* Remove S/M/L and confusing generic names. To achieve this, you can nominate a price for the service e.g. Stylecut & Blowdry $80 then add "long hair plus $20" etc. Don't list 50 different types of treatments just say Treatments $20 -$50. you can give the details when you do your consultation.

- *Main Services & Packages Prominent.* Only have the most popular services on the list, and your main service packages.

- *Available for Clients 24/7* ie. Printed, in the window, to takeaway & Show, Online. Make sure all the information about your salon is on the Pricelist. Contact details, social media, Opening Hours, Your Specialist Skills, Charity you support. Make Potential Clients Like you. Don't put your cancellation policy on the price list, You think I'm Joking, I've seen it done. Absolutely no negatives, no mister cool or nothing intimidating, should be on this, just Happy.

- *Highlight Demographic Specific Value:* Your Pricelist must only appeal to the target demographic that you most want to attract. If you've chosen 35-55 year old Women wanting ShortHair and Colour, don't put "we specialise in Dreadlocks" on your pricelist. Don't Laugh.

Your job as a business owner is to make sure you attract and retain clients and ensure that your price point is greater than your calculated Seat Time Target. That's all.

COMMON STRATEGIES.

Strategies vary from business to business. Factors that decide which strategy is best to use depend on a more than differing influence. We have spent most of our time discussing our target demographic, however the stage that your business sits within its life cycle will also affect the type of strategy you choose. During the course of this chapter I will explain some of the common strategies used. Many of them are best used in different phases of your businesses life cycle.

LIFECYCLE OF A BUSINESS

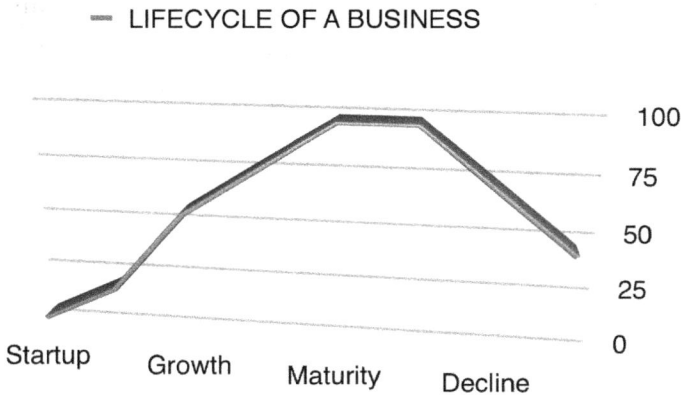

It's important to know where your business is situated and to gather some knowledge about the lifecycle of a business. This will be a great help in planning your strategy. Don't fear if you are in decline. You probably only need a little reinvention to kick start your business, the main thing is that you have identified the situation. There is a stage called rebirth.

How does one Salon charge more than another?

We often ask owners what makes their salon better than the salon across the road? Almost always the answer is 'our stylists are better than theirs'. It's a little hard to fathom, as their stylists have done the same training, had the same experience and worked in other salons around the area. The majority of stylists in the industry do little or no additional training after their basic TAFE or college education. When they do, it's normally just enough to satisfy the basic client needs. The difference between the overall skill from one salon to the next is negligible. In our experience the skill of the stylist only matters where the salon has a distinct education culture and that fact is marketed heavily. The salon has an advantage and they attract clients because of this advantage. These types of salons are in the minority.

I have noted over the years that the busiest staff member in most salons is the most caring person, the best groomed or the best looking stylist. Not necessarily the highest skilled or most experienced stylist.

So, why is it that one salon is always packed? It's probably not simply advertising or social media content. Although that does help attract clients, it doesn't necessarily keep them coming. The price will definitely not be a consideration. When a salons strategy is, to place as many value based service point as possible in their offering, clients will return and recommend to people of similar demographic. Here are some of these service points.

- The Salon management understands what their clients value.

- They demonstrate additional skills in the services they offer, and they can deliver them.

- Ambience, ie room temperature lighting, music and decor are exactly what the client wants.

- Culture, attitude, helpfulness or friendliness within the salon.

- They simply run to time.

- Perhaps they do all these well and their competitors do not.

They probably charge more for their services than anyone else, but they couldn't charge what they do if they didn't have the air conditioner at the right temperature or the music didn't match the ambience the clients expect.

Not that long ago, I opened a salon in a beach side suburb of Sydney, in a Heritage Building. On opening night we had a wine tasting to determine which wine our clients preferred. Over the first few weeks of business we surveyed our clients and asked them about the temperature of the rooms, the music they liked to hear when at the salon, the refreshments they wanted and which room they liked to be seated in. It was never about price always about the experience. Our prices were high for the area but not for the Sydney CBD, our focus was on the client's experience. The salon was always full.

After about three years as my workload increased, I spent most of my time in one of my other salons where our office was located. All the policies and procedures were in place and I felt confident all would be fine. However, as per usual, the staff took the easiest way in each situation (i.e. laziest).

They changed the temperature of the rooms, played their own music, bought cheap wines, and crammed clients together in a room near the desk so they wouldn't have to walk to the phone. They wouldn't follow salon procedures. Suddenly, as a result of their 'I'll do it my way attitude', the salon income plummeted, it was almost impossible to regain what we had lost. Each time I left the salon to return to the office the staff would simply reset the temperature, and the music and carry on for their own benefit, not the clients.

After I asked the team to only play the music provided, one staff member confronted me and told me in no uncertain terms, 'If I didn't let them play the music they liked, I would have a salon full of unhappy and unmotivated staff, who would consider working elsewhere'. My answer should have been, "If you don't play the music the clients like, there will be no need for staff".

Two factors were at play in the downturn in this business. The first and most important one was, the changes the staff made did not reflect what our clients valued. Therefore the clients didn't believe that were getting value for money. The second factor, that is a major problem when you expand your business, 'when the cats away the mice will play'.

Eventually we were forced to move our office back to our flagship salon and we gradually regained our reputation and client base. It took a variety of strategies over a period of time to achieve our rebuild.

OTHER STRATEGIES USED BY SALONS

Not all of the following strategies will suit every salon, and I don't necessarily suggest that these price models should be used. This is by no means a complete list, however, we've listed many of the core pricing strategies most often used in the hair & beauty industry. By now you should have a reasonably accurate idea of your pricing needs. By looking at the following strategies, you will be able to apply these to your price strategy at various times during your business lifecycle. This will further increase your profit or market share. REMEMBER, when you use any of these strategies, you cannot go below your Cost + Margin seat time.

These price strategies represent only a few of the myriad of possibilities that could be applied to any business, but they are at the core of most strategies. You should at least understand these core strategies and be able to apply them or a combination of them from time to time over the life of your business. You may also to choose not to apply any of them, but this is a case of 'you only know what you know'. By arming yourself with this knowledge, you will have a greater understanding of which strategy may or may not apply to your salon's situation.

PRICE SEGMENTATION

Segmentation is a refining of the 20-255 rule. You'll hear people talk about the 80-20 rule. This is a revision of it.

In an article published in the Harvard Business Review, Cooper and Kaplan reported the astonishing case of a company which analysed its client profitability and discovered that the famous 20-80 rule had to be revised. This rule originally suggested that 80% of profits came from 20% of clients.

In fact, a 20-225 rule was actually operating: 20% of clients were generating 225% of profits. The middle 70% of clients were hovering around the break-even point, and 10% of clients were losing 125% of profits. An analysis of your client profitability will help you understand which services you should focus on.

My point here is, if you focus on the clients that make you the most profit, you would lose a large portion of your existing clients and still make the same profit.

This segmentation involves targeting client behaviours, focusing on the value that clients are willing to pay for. Then deciding if you segmentation is fair, and monitoring your strategy to determine if it is being positively embraced by your target clients.

You should make a list of your clients from most profitable to least. Most computer programs will be able to perform this task. Define what your most profitable clients desire and reconfigure the services that your least profitable clients use. This will instantly increase your profits and serve as a reminder not to market to people in future who don't adequately value what you offer.

To set a pricing strategy that maximises profit (or at least increase profit), you must use some sort of price segmentation. After all, not all clients have the same willingness to pay for the services you offer. You make more money when you let people who are willing to pay more, actually pay more.

But is this fair? Is it fair that we charge some people one price and other people a lower price? Do you like it when you pay a price, and find out that someone else bought it cheaper?

Fairness is in the mind of the client. Every client determines whether or not he or she has been fairly treated. Every person has their own sense of fairness. However, there are many examples where it appears we have consensus on what is fair.

Let's look at some examples:

- Students, lower price at a cinemas / fair

- Old-aged pensioners cheaper bus travel / fair

- Holiday-makers pay less than businessmen for airfare / fair

- Paying more for cold drinks on hot days than on cold days / unfair

- Paying more to check your bags on an airline, / unfair

The previous examples show that in Price segmentation, there seem to be three criteria which make something 'fair.'

It is to a businesses advantage to segment their clients and charge them different prices, but if you want to avoid client protests, pay attention to following three rules.

- The segmented price is a discount to one group, not a surcharge to the other group.

- The pricing rules are known to the clients. The clients have learned to play by them.

- The rules do not change. If they do change, they had better change in the clients' favour.

OFF PEAK PRICING:

Off-peak pricing is used to spread the flow of clients when you have obvious peak times. For example If you are unable accommodate any more clients on a Saturday, you could offer reduced prices for those clients who are able to have their service down at a time where your salon has low traffic.

I often advise salon owners to create an off peak ticket for their premium colour package, and seek out colour package clients during peak periods who maybe retirees or shift workers etc. These off peak tickets are valid at the specific low traffic times and provide the client with a substantial discount, but not less than the cost plus margin Price. The advantage here it is that we have included downtime into our price so the majority of income from the off peak ticket is profit, is also allows us to easily fill the appointment that has now become vacant during our peak periods. It is important that you only target very profitable services such as your premium colour package.

MARKET PRICE

We discussed market pricing earlier, but here are a few more general points on the effect on your thought process when you focus on price. Many people believe that when the client and salon owner agree on a price, then the market has arrived at the optimal price. This is not strictly true.

What it means is the client and salon owner agreed on a price at that point in time. The salon owner might be desperate to get some cash flow simply to make payroll. The salon owner almost feels sick when implementing such a low offer, and worries about the fact the salon is running into the red next month. Things will be better by then. Hopefully!

Meanwhile, the client now has an expectation that she can always get discounts if she pushes hard enough. She makes a mental note to ask for the same discount next appointment. After all, she got the distinct impression the salon owner has even more room to move.

Getting pricing right is more than two parties agreeing on a price at a particular point in time. Pricing is also strategic. Pricing is about the long-term sustainability of a business. But ultimately, pricing is about value not price.

SKIM PRICING

Skimming is the process of setting high prices based on perceived value, well above the cost+margin price. Instead of basing your prices on your competition, Skim Pricing is when you set a much higher price than your competitors.

In order to set pricing in this way, your clients need to perceive that your service provides them with greater benefits than they will find elsewhere. This is the main principle of Perceived Value Pricing

This strategy can be employed in emerging markets, where certain clients will always want a famous stylist or the newest, trendiest product available. It also works well in a mature market, where clients have already realised the value of your service and are willing to pay for what you offer. Surprisingly, skimming also works in declining markets, as your diehard clients are willing to pay more for what they see as an older, but superior service with a dwindling supply.

It can easily be argued that many clients also gain social value, via "ego caressing" when paying a high price, as they boast about having something exclusive e.g. "stylist of the year".

In order to skim price, you need to offer something the client can't easily get elsewhere. The client must place a high value upon your service.

Stylists with proven reputations or a celebrity clientele can use skim pricing, although maintaining a reputation over and above everyone else in crowded, maturing markets can be difficult. Competitors will soon enter the space, offering similar value.

The benefit of Skim Pricing is that you get to pick off the price-insensitive top of the market clients.

The downside is that other competitors can move into the price gap, slightly beneath the skim level, then bump up the value they offer, in order to challenge the skim price competitor.

It is only so long before the market leader is forced to drop prices, refine their value proposition, or collapse.

Skim Pricing can lead to a rapid erosion of market share if the leader does not stay well ahead of the market in terms of providing value. In this case because you are priced well above your Cost + Margin seat time, you will have lots of room to move.

Neutral Pricing

Neutral pricing is when you set your pricing at a comparable level to your competitors.

In a neutral strategy, the prices are set by the general market, with your prices equal to your competitors' prices

You would use this pricing method if you wanted clients to consider other aspects, besides price, when they contemplate a purchase, ie. A package or bundle where a blow dry is added to a haircut is the same price as your competitors haircut only.

Neither salon wants to engage in a price war, so they will keep layering on more value in order to make their offer more compelling.

If either salon started cutting prices in order to compete, then they'd have a 'race to the bottom' problem. This market sector retains value for all players, so long as they deliver genuine value to clients.

Since the strategy is determined by the market, not on your product, your company, or the value of either, you're not going to gain any additional market share. Essentially, neutral pricing is the safe way to play the pricing game but not necessarily the most profitable.

Neutral Pricing is an especially good pricing model to use if you want your clients to focus on the features of the offer. If you offer more features for the same price, you will likely win. This strategy is not recommended unless you have a good handle on your seat time calculations. Being able to monitor your seat time is essential when using this pricing model.

PENETRATION PRICING

A penetration strategy is a price war. This strategy goes for the deepest price cuts, driving at every moment to have your price the lowest on the market. In some forms Penetration pricing is illegal in Australia.

Penetration strategies only work in one of the four business lifecycle periods, Growth. During Growth, your sales are continuing to expand, as your clients want the newest product, but still a product that has already been tested by others in the emerging period.

This is when your sales units will be highest. A penetration strategy works here, and only here, because you are attracting clients to a new but proven service with a low cost re-production. You're developing relationships with new clients willing to try your service but their focus is on a lower price. This strategy was evident with Keratin Straightening, Moroccan / Argan Oil and Foiling. As the market has expanded suppliers came in and heavily cut prices to gain market share. Consequently the price has dropped, these services and products now sell lower than one quarter of their original market price.

Penetration strategies fail in the other business lifecycle periods by leaving possible profits in the hands of the clients. In a startup market, your service is brand new and clients who want it first, should (and will) pay for that right.

In a mature market, a price war will simply start the process of endless and useless competition, destroying your profit margin.

In a declining market, only those who still must have your service will purchase it, and just like in an emerging period, they should (and will) pay for that right.

Recognising the lifecycle that your business is in will help you decide which pricing strategy works best for your salon. This is essential knowledge for any pricing manager.

COMPETITIVE PRICING

In most market pricing situations, your competitors' prices will tell you what you can or should be charging. Assessing how your service compares to your competitors, and understanding the value your target clients put on the different features and benefits you offer will also give you a good idea of what your own offer should be worth.

Setting your prices near to those of your competitors is a safe strategy because potential clients won't rule your services out immediately for being too expensive. You'll also avoid the risk of starting a price war by undercutting rivals.

To compete using a competitive pricing strategy, you must have a very accurate and up to date knowledge of your "Seat Time". By focusing on your competitors price point, you could leave yourself very close to your break even point. As with Neutral and Market Pricing it is suggested you only investigate these models as a guide, to ensure you are not undercharging

PREMIUM PRICING

If you have a grip on your market prices, it's tempting to set yours just a little lower to give yourself a competitive edge. In fact, setting a slightly higher price is often a better pricing strategy.

In the minds of many clients, a higher price suggests better quality and any reduction in turnover caused by high prices can be more than offset by larger profit margins. If it doesn't work, you can always reduce your prices to a more competitive level.

Premium Pricing can be effective where there are barriers to your competitors, if you have an exclusive service or product or loyal clients, for example.

Smaller businesses with higher unit costs, can't afford to compete on price alone. They need to focus on adding value through excellent client service etc, so as to create a service that can be sold for a Premium Price.

Psychological pricing & Odd Value Pricing

Using the retailer's tactic of selling services for $99 instead of $100 can be useful if price is an essential part of clients' buying decisions. Some clients perceive odd value prices like this as being more attractive.

This hypothesis suggests that clients perceive the difference between $1.99 and $3.00 to be closer to $2.01 than to $1.01 because their judgments are anchored on the left-most digit.

The theory of psychological pricing is controversial. Some studies show that buyers, even young children, have a very sophisticated understanding of true cost and relative value. Other researchers claim that this ignores the non-rational nature of the phenomenon and that acceptance of the theory requires belief in a subconscious level of thought processes, a belief that economic models tend to deny or ignore.

Now that many clients are used to odd pricing (e.g. $29.99), some restaurants, high-end retailers and salons psychologically price in even numbers (eg 30 or 32) in an attempt to reinforce their brand image of quality and sophistication. They often remove the $ sign to further soften the impact.

Psychological pricing suggests that it is often easy to move prices up to the next psychological 'barrier.' If the price is $55.00, it might be possible to raise it to $59.99 without difficulty. The key is not adding a digit or changing the leftmost number, e.g., $59.00 can go to $59.99, but not to $60.

You can break out fees formerly included in the price. This is a practical application of psychological pricing. Suppose we sell a cut, colour and toner for $199. If we want/need to raise prices, we'd have to cross the $200 'barrier' and likely lose sales. So instead we keep the price at $199, but remove the toner from the package and charge as an option for $19 we've kept the price under the barrier and increased the price to the market segment that doesn't care about price or those who need the service. We then add it back in at a later date when the rest of the market has caught up.

Odd Value pricing works well when used as a strategy in conjunction with service bundling where you can increase an individual item but keep your service bundle at the same price.

SERVICE BUNDLING

Bundling services is one of the most effective and commonly used methods in the hair industry. Similar to loss leader you can reduce the price of a service and bundle it with another to raise ticket value. An extremely simple example is this. Suppose a haircut is $50 and a Blowdry is $50 you could bundle and charge $95 this has many effects on your business,. Firstly by increasing your ticket value, secondly decreasing your seat time therefore your hourly costs, and thirdly by potentially attracting more clients through competitive pricing.

However you do it, ensure that the transition between price points makes sense. The transition can't appear arbitrary. The more expensive bundle is more expensive because it has more input costs, demonstrably delivers more value, or both.

Salons who get this wrong typically create arbitrary price settings between bundles. There isn't a lot of distinction in terms of value between the jumps, or the core offering is not included at the low level.

Salons will typically put their core offerings in every package, and then add 'nice-to-have' features at higher price levels. All clients will want the core offering. Price sensitive clients will settle for the core offering and nothing else. Value clients will likely add the nice-to-haves so long as these extras provide the value they seek. Once a client is on board at the low-value level, then they may wish to add extras next time they visit, after the value has been demonstrated.

In the right salon environment, this could be an excellent pricing model and it is currently used by many software companies. Their core product, if it is commodity, is often free or priced extremely low. This hooks you into using it, but doesn't cost the company much to deliver. It is used as a loss leader sales-tool.

If you want more benefits, then you move up the scale to higher price points. It's very difficult for competitors to compete with this strategy, because the core offering is low priced and the switching cost, whilst possibly not high, still exists.

An example is offering one free child's haircut when your client has a Cut and Blowdry, but only if they rebook. The client wants the free child's haircut, so they become loyal to your salon and you get maximum profit because of the four to six week rebooking. On your salon price list, you should place children's haircuts with a high value, maybe $5-$7 above the market, so that if the client brings in a second or third child you shift them up the scale and increase your profits. You could also make this offer only available with entry level stylists.

In order to compete, competitors must offer better services or more features, and due to their ignorance, they will probably lower prices.

LOSS LEADER

This involves selling a product at a low or even loss making price. Although you may not make a profit selling this product, you could attract clients who will also buy other, more profitable services. A great example is offering a product or service at, or under cost, when your client purchases a particular high price package.

'BUT WAIT THERE'S MORE'.

Similar to a loss leader strategy, this model involves charging a premium price for advanced or related products and services. Then offering another one, or a basic product or service, free of charge or at a very low price the idea is that the initial products is sold at a premium price.

The catch is offering an additional feature or service that really adds value. Take your time before springing this model on clients.

Many businesses try to extract premium price without creating value over multiple engagements with their client. You need to give the right offers to the right clients at the right times to be successful.

The $5 Product is a perfect example of a good "but wait there's more" marketing Promotion. This is how it works. With our Premium cut and colour package, clients were given an incentive to rebook. Their Haircut would be free if they rebooked with-in a 4 to 6 week time frame. That sounds simple but after a while clients were ringing with all sorts of excuses and pushing out their appointment. Of course our stylists said Ok to the request and the clients return rate started to blow out, thus defeating the purpose of the free cut promotion. To counter this we offered our package clients "but wait there's more". The clients could purchase, one shampoo or conditioner for $5, provided they hadn't changed their appointment booking.

Because there was more than one condition and more than one reward, we regained our return client rate but our retail sales also improved. It is amazing but most clients couldn't stand to only buy one shampoo they had to also buy the matching conditioner and while they were at it they got some styling products, after all they did save $25 on the $5 product.

Our salon had a high stock turnover and because we only dealt with one product company, we became a major account to our supplier and received very good wholesale prices on our retail products. Our limited variety of premium retail products cost about 33% of the r.r.p. I could sell two products for ($40+$5) with a cost around $26. The fact I could also get another 4+ visits per year at $295 from each client made this promotion very profitable for our salon.

TIERED PRICING & CHOICE STRATEGY

Businesses must innovate in order to retain current and capture new clients. Relying on price increases alone to drive growth is unlikely to work unless clients cannot get the service elsewhere.

One solution is to provide multiple products or service levels. If some buyers are genuinely price oriented, that's fine, but they get the lowest service level. Contrary to popular opinion, most clients are actually value oriented, and will choose higher value services, so long as they perceive genuine value, or can be shown by you that there is a value difference.

One price methodology involves creating three or four levels. One low priced offer, one mid priced offer, and one high priced offer.

Many clients, when faced with the 'choice of three' will pick the middle offer. Salons often price this way. They'll have one or two stylist with prices at a very high end price and give them a title to prove their experience e.g. 'Artistic Director or Creative

Director'. They will group other stylists in a mid range called Senior Stylists or something similar, and place them in a neutral or competitive price range. The third group will be emerging stylists or entry level stylists that have not long finished their basic training and need a clientele. Most clients will use the end two points as price guides, and buy somewhere in the middle.

Try pricing your top level Stylist at skim pricing levels. Include all the bells-and-whistles in the service. Most people won't pay this price, but between this and the lowest price stylist, clients will set their expectations. The middle bundle is actually your full price offering, possibly neutrally priced against your competitors, because neutrally priced clients may see it as the sensible middle ground compromise. Funnily enough, you'll be surprised at how many people still go for the top price option! The entry level stylist is a great way to help your budding stylists build a clientele. The prices set at this level would ideally be at your seat time price and no lower. As they move to the senior stylist level most of their clients will follow them, providing you have given some notice. Make sure that you still have an emerging stylist level so that your price sensitive clients can be retained. Don't rule out introducing a transition level, a fourth level, to ease price sensitive clients along.

Payment Plans, Memberships & Loyalty Programs

Businesses must endeavour to retain and collect the maximum income from their clients. Payment plans or memberships are a fantastic way to do this.

I developed a payment plan for mine and a number of other salons that guaranteed over 25% of our weekly income, even if the clients did not have an appointment.

The upside of a payment plan or membership is that you have a constant cashflow. The downside is that your cashflow is levelled out and your admin costs are increased.

There are laws governing these sorts of arrangements, the fitness industry laws are a great guide to learning what you can and cannot do.

I'll explain briefly how our payment plan worked. We offered two packages. The less expensive package aimed at filling our quietest time. By buying the package, clients only received a small discount on their Cut and Colour, but they received substantial savings on their retail products and other services in the salon. We offered hair and beauty services so it was easy to cross promote.

The upside for us was that all clients paid for a return cut & colour every 5 weeks and they bought retail and they were committed to our beauty department for services they didn't use previously

OFF PEAK Hair Package
$36 per week
$5 extra for Less than 5 week frequency
Between 9:00am and 2:00pm
Monday to Thursday

PEAK Hair Package
$44 per week
$8 extra for Less than 5 week frequency
Available any time during trading hours.

The services included in our Cut and Colour Packages are:
The colour service of your choice, 1/2 or full head foils, semi or tint plus your Haircut and Blowdry, Shampoo, conditioner and after colour treatment.

We will Direct Debit weekly, commencing approximately 1 week after you sign the Direct Debit form. You will receive a copy of the signed form.
A once only admin fee of $5.50 will be charged by paysmart on the first debit.

You can rebook at intervals required to keep your hair in premium condition. The intervals between appointments can not be closer than 5 weeks unless you have included the frequency supplement in your plan. Your stylist will advise you. Most clients return between 5 and 8 weeks

On the day of your Cut & Colour, you pay nothing for the services in your Package. You will also receive a voucher pack that will give you discounts of approximately $650 for other hair and beauty services. These can be used at anytime during salon hours. We will issue a new voucher pack every January. Clients will automatically receive 20% off all Retail Products in the salon.

BEST INTERESTS OF THE CLIENT

It might be in the best interests of your client to pay higher prices if this means the value they seek can be reliably delivered on an on-going basis. If your business is run into the ground due to price cutting, then where will the clients get the services they really do value.?

Part of the process of getting pricing right is client education. Demonstrate so they can see the value. Demonstrate what is involved in arriving at your price points. For example have logical Price Lists that show individual prices and package discounts.

Knowing what price to set is knowing what the client values, or helping clients see value where previously they saw none.

Always ask questions and refine your services based on the answers to the following questions.

- Do I need to change how I present my existing services in order to demonstrate value?

- Do I need to change my services to meet the market?

There's More To Price Than Price. Some clients accept that buying on price alone may be a poor strategy. Clients are likely to have a switching price. The way to counter this, is to know your value, relative to the competition. You can always match with a lower price, as long as the client accepts that you will be reducing your features to match those on offer from your competitors. The Client will either accept your discounted offer, meaning price really was an issue, or accept your higher full value price, meaning value was the main issue.

You must also have calculated an accurate seat time and stick to it. Some clients simply aren't worth having. The minute you raise prices, they go back out and look for another salon offering lower prices.

In service businesses, one way of preventing a client from trying to get the expensive bundle for the low cost price is to be transparent about your pricing. Yes, they can have the extras, but they involve X more seat time. How much additional seat time do they wish to purchase? This is transparent. It makes logical sense. There is no arguing with this position, as everyone understands, that time is money.

DISCOUNTS, SALES & OFFERS

Think positively and profitably,

Use discounting as a short term tactic,

not as a long term strategy

DISCOUNTING:

Before you close your mind and pull down your shutters, before you jump on your high horse and tell us that you never discount, you need to think deeper about discounting, and its possible applications, and effects on your salon business.

Most salons discount and don't even know it. If you didn't raise your prices when you should have last year, you just started discounting. If you haven't raised your prices in the last five years you are discounting your prices by at least 20%.

Discounts, having a sale, client promotions, offers or coupon selling, loyalty programs or not raising your prices, are all discount strategies and tactics. I'm sure, each of you use one of these or something similar.

Lowering your prices might produce increased sales and more cash, when cash is tight. Discounting can be a tempting quick fix. But like most quick fixes, there is a downside. The danger comes when discounting becomes a long-term strategy, rather than a short-term tactic. You can quickly and easily, shift new client focus from, value to price, putting yourself firmly entrenched in the Marketing Price Model.

Effective Discount strategies, that offer specially reduced prices can be a powerful tool. This could be a discount, for making multiple purchases of the same or similar services, or you could offer bundle discounts to encourage multiple service appointments. You may also be able to make these more profitable through lower costs by reducing stock or service time.

Be careful. If you discount too often, clients may question your full-rate pricing or see you as a cheap option, making it difficult to charge full-rate prices in the future.

Think about it. When you spend more time offering deals, than you do explaining why clients should want to use your services, you are perilously close to saying, 'Our services are not good enough to sell on their merits at full price.'

What I'm really saying is, messages that give emotional or rational reasons for clients to buy, are the key to building your business and brand.

You should not say never discount. We offer discounts all the time. Our discounts are planned, and used to drive clients or tie clients to an addition or future purchase.

A steady stream of discounts will cheapen your brand and actually drive away your less price sensitive clients. Remember that the clients who buy most from a promotion are often your best clients, who would have bought anyway. Discounting, using bundles or packages, should clearly give clients benefits for return bookings, or additional offerings, like Toners and Treatments, or for upsetting to a Premium Service.

WHEN & HOW TO USE DISCOUNTS SALES & OFFERS

There are a hundred and one ways you can use sales, offers, discounts and deals to retain and build a clientele.

I'm not saying all of these apply,Let's take a look at some of the most popular ways to approach these sales ideas.

Monthly Service Highlighting. These are traditional sales used to increase income and promote a particular service. Sales such as a January Promotion, 'Half Price Scalp Massage' with every Cut and Blow-dry, or "Toner only $10", save $15 with every Colour Service. These promotions are used to increase revenues and highlight potential add on services. If clients like these add on services your staff could rebook the service with an incentive next visit. Potentially the toner or scalp massage could become an integral part of the normal service plan or package in future months

Prelaunch Offers. If you're still in the prelaunch stage of your business or maybe even launching a new product or service, you can use prelaunch offers to help drive traffic and increase client awareness. You could pre-sell appointments for the new service at reduced rates.

Holiday Season Offers. Mother's Day, Easter, Christmas and New years are the obvious big ones, but the whole year is sprinkled with holidays and celebrations that you can use to increase revenue with offers.

Offers for Liking, Following, Sharing On Social Media. One of the hardest parts of running a salon is getting word out. Giving visitors and clients an incentive to share your salon with their social circles can be an effective way to create some inexpensive word of mouth.

Text, Email/Newsletter Subscription Offer. Don't Hide your email address like everyone else. As you probably already know, building an email list is extremely important for your salon business. By providing an offer in exchange for visitors emails address, not only increases the chance of a conversion, but you also get their email address, providing you with the opportunity to market new products and offers to them in the future. A great tactic is to text last minute offers or run a competitions that require an email reply.

Exclusive Social Offers. Exclusive offers on your social networks can be a great way to build a strong relationship with those that follow you as well as provide a reason for new people to follow and subscribe to your social channels This will allow you to market to them in the future. Good for last minute to fill downtime. If you find you have downtime during the current day send a morning email or post, offering discounted services to fill the empty afternoon appointments.

Referral Offers. People are much more likely to purchase from you if referred by a friend or family member. Use this to your advantage and use offers to encourage referrals. You can choose to give a deal to the person referring, the person being referred or both.

First Time Shopper Offer. Providing a new client offer could be all thats needed for a first-time visitor to be converted to a regular paying client. A phone follow-up to ask how everything was with the first visit is a great way to personalise the relationship. Beware, some of the these tactics could leave loyal clients unhappy, if there is no offer for them.

Volume Offers. An offer based on the total value of a combined service is an effective up selling tactic, designed to encourage clients to spend more and increasing your average ticket. Similar to Bundling services but not a formal package on your price list this is an effective way to undercut your opposition and still make a substantial profit by encouraging add-on services, eg if you spend $150 you receive a discount on all additional purchases.

Client Loyalty Offers. Rewarding client loyalty can help build an even stronger bond, while also only providing discounts to clients that already spend money in your salon. The reward can be as simple as sending your best clients a personal email, with a discounted service offer, or using automated email marketing, via an app or CMP that sends out email offers when someone makes a certain number of purchases from your store. A widely used client loyalty program, that gives points for frequent visits. Try not to simply give a free service after 10 visits i.e 10% discount, this sort of offer is not that exciting and not likely to maintain loyalty, you have effectively reduced your prices by 10%, without any increased commitment. It would be better to have a range of rewards that your client may choose from, vouchers for service you want to promote, or Products etc. it is better to give extra rather than lower your price

Internet Exit Intent Offer. If you website is up to speed, and Clients can buy or book online, sometimes all it takes to convert a potential client to a client is a last second offer before they leave. An Exit Intent Offer will popup just as your visitor is about to leave your website or close the tab, presenting them with a final offer to purchase.

Re-Targeting Offer. Re-Targeting offers are effective because they're only shown to people who have been into your salon, so the client already knows who you are. The offer could be, a discount on a Retail product if the client rebooks for a higher price service bundle. These offers serve as a reminder to come back and the offer serves as an incentive to purchase additional items or return.

Building client loyalty, to increase salon revenue is the short term tactic of implementing an offer or discount, definitely not right for every salon, but with an understanding of your brand, a clear plan in mind, plus a little experimentation you are most able to utilise offers and discounts to meet your objectives.

CLIENT LOYALTY.

Everyone loves a deal. So you'd think your regular clients would be thrilled to receive a discount. And they probably will be at first. Think about what attracted your best client to begin with, it was probably was and should be much more than the price.

Factors like product variety, personal service or a reputation for quality are what keeps your clients coming back. If they see you lowering prices too often, they may assume you've lowered your standards or that your business is not that popular. A steady stream of discounts will cheapen your brand, and may actually drive away your best clients.

Discounting also attracts price shoppers, an entirely different and fickle audience. They'll only be with you as long as you keep discounting. This is not how you should be marketing.

SELECTIVITY:

You can avoid discounting by promoting the real value of your product or service. This can include excellent client service, a wide or exclusive product line, high quality and an on-time appointment record. If you discount for one client, you'll more than likely have to discount for other clients and prospective clients. The salon may end up trapped selling at a lower price permanently. That's even worse news for your cash flow. To avoid being stuck in permanent discount mode, you can segment your offer, eg. to a one-time only discount or a first-time client discount.

If you can segment your clients into different service markets, it's easier to offer a discount to one segment without having to offer it to everyone. For example, you could segment to a specific group e.g. Off peak discounts to colour package clients, Blow-dry clients, Foil Clients, Long Hair Clients etc and make offers only to clients who use that segment. Or Offer a one off discount if the take services from another segment. eg A cut and tint client receives a discount for upgrading to foils.

A great example of selective discounting is, when introducing a price rise, display the new price list but don't apply it to your current loyal clients. The new price is delayed and slowly introduced to your loyal clients, because they are "loyal and have supported you business", the new higher price, is immediately applied to new clients and those who don't rebook.

TIMING.

Discounting is a good way to clear out seasonal retail stock, and clients have come to expect after-holiday and end-of-season bargains. Discounting at the end of season or after major events ie Christmas, can be your friend in these situations. It's a way to get rid of products that aren't selling well or can't be returned. Linking the sale to a rarely sold or new season service is even better.

Discounting can also attract new clients who haven't used your product or service before. The downside is you can't predict how much of the business will return, and you may offend long-time clients who see newcomers getting a better deal.

Study your clients cashflow through out the year. Holiday time might not be the best time for a price increase

PERSPECTIVES ON DISCOUNTING

How do your clients, employees and competitors react to discounting? It's helpful to consider their perspectives.

Clients: If some Clients always expect a discount, are they the type of Client you really want? Avoid clients who consistently want to drive you into a lower rate and promise to pay your regular rate next time.

Your Employees: Sometimes your staff can be quick to offer a discount, thinking it's the best way to close a sale, or to keep the client coming back. Often they may be underestimating a client who feels they're already getting a fair price, and the discount isn't necessary. If a client or prospective client, can't pay your price or doesn't want to, is this the type of client you really want?

Competitors: When your competitors get wind that you're offering discounts, and you know they will, they may follow suit and soon you'll have a price war. That could mean a downward profit spiral until one of you is out of business. Some of your clients may tell you the competition offered them a lower price. Let them take it. They may be saying the same thing about you.

Think Long-Term.

Don't waste time on clients who will never value what you do. Instead, devote more time to cultivating clients willing to pay what your product or service is worth. Those clients are the ones who will refer you to other good clients. Each time you have price rise, clients and staff will put pressure on you to keep things the same, or make the price rise smaller. Despite the chatter and it may seem counter intuitive, but rather than discounting or holding back your prices, think about raising your prices on a more regularly basis. To maintain valuable employees you will need to give them increased wages, bonuses or commission. As you gain experience and your salon's reputation grows, it only makes sense to raise prices.

Tactics, not Strategy.

A major department store's experience is a cautionary tale of what happens when discounts take over. The chain offered a steady stream of discounts, coupons and sales to compete with other stores. A newly appointed CEO announced a more streamlined policy of across-the-board, everyday savings, he stopped using coupons and ended the daily specials program.

He didn't realise that discounting was so ingrained. Clients didn't like into this new approach and profits suffered because the clients didn't believe that they were being offered a discount any more. In reality, he stopped spoon feeding his clients by not showing them how much they were saving.

Rather than discounting, it may be better to concentrate on the value you offer your clients. That way you'll grow your business without selling yourself short.

Clients will ask for discounts for reasons ranging from paying cash, to spending a lot of money with you, to seeing the service cheaper elsewhere. Is it a good idea to give into their demands or not?

One of the best ways for business owners to solve the discount dilemma is to set up a unified discount program. For example, a volume discount. You could give all clients 10% off services if they spend more than $200 then 15% on services totalling more than $300. Having a pre-existing discount program, advertised on your pricelist, allows you to treat all clients fairly and saves you from having to make markdown decisions on a case-by-case basis. If your team is regularly offer to clients discounts behind your back, advertising this type of volume discount policy will help set specific boundaries for your team.

THE PLUS SIDE TO DISCOUNTING

Discounting only has plus side when, you can calculate, that you will get a better financial return by applying the strategy. I'm mean Calculate not Speculate. If a client receives a discount for rebooking or upgrading, you can calculate the return. If you offer a discount, on a cut a dry to match a competitor, you can only speculate on how much additional business (if any) you will gain. When it seems clear, that a client will go elsewhere unless you give in to a request for a discount, ask yourself how badly you need this particular client? The answer should be, let her go. Granting your clients the discount they request probably won't improve their loyalty to your business. Giving discounts in rare cases can create return business, it can also generate positive word of mouth and build your reputation as a community-minded business owner. Rewarding loyal clients here and there, certainly won't cut that deeply into your bottom line. In fact, giving Seniors or for Those that support certain charities or events could even strengthen your profit by promoting return business and sending new clients your way.

THE MINUS SIDE TO DISCOUNTING

Any time you sell your product or service for lower than your asking price, your profit margin is reduced. If you can hold out, you might be better off waiting for clients who are willing to pay full price.

Even if you tell clients the discount is a one-time occurrence, they may expect it next time. If you refuse, their loyalty to your business might prove fleeting. Only give a discount if you don't mind being asked for more deals in the future.

If some of your loyal clients who aren't getting a discount talk to a client who is, they will wonder why they haven't received the same courtesy. These clients might demand a concession the next time you see them, and you will be forced to comply or else risk losing their business. Many people enjoy sharing the news when they get a good deal. Don't imagine that your clients will be an exception.

HOW DISCOUNTING IMPACTS CLIENT LOYALTY

Think About the Following Examples: In the first photograph, we have a Store offering 20% to 74% Discount.

From the inventory point of view, it's post Christmas and they have to move their seasonal stock. In theory, this seems to be a great accountancy move, all their clients can buy stock greatly reduced and it will certainly attract new clients looking for a bargain.

On the minus side, would you be happy if the shoes you bought for $400 before Christmas are now $104? Would a 20% discount attract you as a new buyer? What does this say about their exclusive stock? Is it really exclusive and high quality, or is it just marked up excessively? Would the client be better shopping at a store that sold discounted shoes all year round? The discount shoe shop and the exclusive shoe shop suddenly appear to wholesale at the same price. Besides that, what does 74% off mean? is it 74% off a $4000 or a $400 pair of shoes? This company just shot themselves in the foot, literally.

In the second example below, the Client is being offered a 50% discount on one product, if they purchase two items at full price. This means that the overall discount will be less than 25%, but to me, this offer seems far more attractive than advertising a 25% discount.

The store is offering a discount for volume and it doesn't offend any loyal clients. It doesn't imply that the quality of the stock is inferior.

It also doesn't indicate that clients should expect continued discounts. The offer is clear and the clients understand their potential saving. Even if the discount went to 100% off your second item for one week only, the store is only giving a maximum of 50% discount.

The third example is an even better way to move sales. Firstly, the store is actually offering a 30% discount, but with clear wording they are telling clients that if they spend $100 they will receive $30 off. This is so much better than offering a 30% discount, money talks, clients can calculate how much they are willing to spend and how much they will save.

Offering 'X' Dollars off a service or money vouchers for services

on the next visit that equate to real cash are a far more tangible way to generate return business or new business without lowering your perceived value. There is no implication that you are operating a discount business. Our tip here is, always avoid using percentages as they mean nothing to potential clients.

RAISING YOUR PRICES

OMG!!!

NOT A PRICE RISE

Striking fear, into the heart of every hairdresser

If we raise our prices, **ALL** of our clients will complain. Maybe they'll all go to another salon!!!, 'Phooey'.

Does anyone actually realise, that if a client says to you, "Oh you've had price rise", that they may be commenting, not necessarily complaining about a "price hike". The last time I raised a salons prices, one of the therapists told us 'ALL' of her clients had complained about the 'price hike', the therapist had serviced 65 clients since the 'price hike', so I decided that the owner should analyse each and every service.

Every client was contacted, only to discover that there was only one 'complaint'. When we contacted that particular client, her comment was, 'I was expecting this months ago, it's been ages since you've increased your prices' I was just commenting on the new price, it wasn't really a complaint. Is it poor Perception of Value, or, Ignorance of Business Protocol, or, low self esteem, that causes this blood curdling fear, of raising prices in all of us. The fear and the most protests more often than not is from our staff.

It is interesting, that in general staff will always want more in their pay packet, but they are reluctant to collect the money from its source (the client). I do understand, that it is difficult to face a client, and talk about a price rise.

The subtle strategy of planning small, regular increases is the most effective, and least offensive way to raise prices. Rather than implementing, an across the board price rise, every two or three years.

Just recently a client of ours moved their salon from an outlying suburb to a location opposite a large Westfield shopping centre. My client had a Beauty Therapist sub-leasing space in their hairdressing salon, she charged her clients around $58 per hour. Just before the move, she decided it was a good time to increase her prices, since her overheads were about to increase. I believe her decision to increase her prices was correct. That was the only correct decision she made.

The price of a one hour service went from $58 to $90 in one foul swoop. Her next marketing sin, was to inform her clients via text message, in a single line of text that simply stated, "on your next visit your facial will be $90". Unfortunately for her, this was the wrong strategy, even $89 would have sounded a little softer. Maybe it wasn't a strategy! She didn't even say, "I'm sorry" or "thanks for supporting me" or give any explanation why the price had to increase.

Over the years, she had built herself a price sensitive clientele, by keeping her prices well below the market. She decided to jump the price close to the perceived market price, with no mention of added value or reward for her price sensitive clients.I don't need to explain what happened to her business.

She was desperate to increase her income. Segmented discounting would have been a better approach in this situation. To soften to blow and ease her clients in, when introducing a price rise, display the new price list, but don't apply it to your current <u>loyal</u> clients. The new price is delayed for them, and slowly introduced, because they are "loyal and have supported you business", the new higher price, is immediately applied to new clients and those who don't rebook.

THE LIFE OF A CLIENT

What is the life of a Client? How many times will a client return to your salon before moving on to another? I cannot recall how many hundreds of times, salon owners have told us that all of "their clients" rebook, or all of "their clients" return. Talk about an ostrich mentality.

Every Salons Client base can be divided into four groups.

a). A core group. Maybe up to 40% that return regularly 4 to 6 weeks.

b). Another quite large group. Again about 40% that comes in sporadically around 8 to 13 week return.

c). Thirdly, those who rarely return.

d). A group of new clients who enter the salon each week.

These new clients, keep the average weekly number of clients more or less stable. Wella Australia did some research a few years ago, and suggested that the average life of a salon client was 6.8 visits. Like most of you, I refused to believe it. At the time we had a very successful salon with very loyal clients.

I was sure Wella must be talking about the cheap poorly skilled salon down the road and not us. So using our computer data we analysed our clients Statistics. By averaging groups A, B & C. Low and behold, our overall client life was only 7.1 visits. just fractionally better than Wella's National Average.

Given this realisation, should any salon owner really care if a dozen clients leave when they raise their prices?

Your Job as a Salon owner, is to nurture your two core client groups by improving their return rate and helping them understand the value you are providing for them.

If you concentrated on this task, if you could extended the average client life by three additional visits. This focus will increase the number of weekly clients and also your profit by nearly 20% within a few months.

PRICE, QUALITY OR SATISFACTION

The Rockefeller Corporation Studied why clients stopped visiting their current salon. When asking each client personally, they found the following:

- *1% The client died or became ill*

- *3% The client moved away*

- *5% The Client had a friend who provides the service*

- *9% The client is lost to a competitor through a changed circumstance. (other than price)*

- *14% The Client was dissatisfied with some aspect of the service*

- *68% The Client Believes that you do not care about them*

Notice how price and quality are absent from the client reasons for leaving list.

The fact is, that most defections (82%) are a result of human failings and perceptions of indifference, rather than price or technical quality.

When did you last, examine the internal functions of your business that relate to personal attitude, and then price for profit? We should be wise about raising our prices. Of course, there are some risks to raising prices, but prices rises are a fact of life. It is remotely Possible, although I've never heard of a case in our industry, where someone has priced too high and sold themselves out.

You need to raise prices on a regular basis as part of managing your business. If you never raise your prices, you won't be in business for long. Constant monitoring of your price and your costs ensures you are both competitive in the market and that you generate the profit your business needs.

WHEN & HOW

One strategy, used by less informed managers, is to wait, and only raise prices when competitors are raising prices theirs. Competitors raising their prices is a safe, but good signal that the market can and will support a price increase for your services as well.

Another is to raise prices when your clients start commenting about what a great value your services are, that may indicate you're charging too low a price.

Review your costs and raise your prices regularly. Try not to make changes at the start of a New Financial or Calendar Year, often this is when your clients are experiencing cash flow problems themselves. Stagger Price Rises in different service segments throughout the year.

If you study the cash flow, and holiday times, throughout the year, one could suggest that October is the best time to have a price rise. This is when clients are least committed financially and their next appointment will probably their Christmas visit so they really don't want to try a new hairdresser on that appointment.

Don't raise prices all at once. Raise prices in small increments over two, three or more price increases over the a year.

Don't raise prices across the board. Be discreet. In today's economy, you need to raise prices where you think your client can't see there has been an increase. A great example is to introduce a higher-priced 'new or improved' service while making older and cheaper ones obsolete. Clients may not notice price increases if they are only for certain services and not for others.

Make sure your decision is focused on why you are raising prices. Is it simply to make more money? or is it because your costs have increased?

THINGS TO CONSIDER

Weigh up the risks. But don't let the risks blind you, you must have price rises. How many clients would you be likely to lose if your prices went up? Some clients are motivated mainly by value for money. Would the loss of clients be compensated by the price rise? Would a price increase put off potential Clients?

Will your competitors be able to capitalise on your price increases, by offering, or being seen to offer, cheaper alternatives. Remember if your marketing to your specific target group, and your services have a high level of value for this group, competitor capitalisation opportunity will be low.

Work out what your profit per sale would be if you increased your prices. Maybe you could afford to lose a few sales but still increase your overall profitability. Even though turnover can go down, profitability can rise. Some of your major overheads like wages and stock may reduce.

If you are left with no other choice but to put your prices up, don't be afraid to do so. The risks posed to your business are far worse by leaving your prices as they are for fear of upsetting a client.

Reducing Prices

As discussed earlier, you should never take the decision to lower prices lightly. Low prices are often perceived to go hand-in-hand with poor-quality and poor service. Is this the image you want to create for your business? Be mindful, if you don't raise your prices when you actually should, you are in effect lowering your prices. Your clients perception of your business could be lowered as you drop down the price scale. Lower prices will never attract a profitable number of new clients.

A better plan to build up sales, would be to concentrate on building profits rather than cutting prices to build up sales.

In most circumstances, your clients decide to buy from you because of the benefits or value that you offer, and how that marries up with your price. It is rare for their decision to be based solely on the price. Odd number pricing is possibly the only time reducing prices **may** be acceptable e.g. $89.99 instead of $90.

TACTICS

If you're starting a business, carefully consider your pricing strategy before you start. If you own an established business you can improve your profitability through regular pricing reviews and varying your price rise strategy.

When setting your prices you must make sure that your cost + margin price is correct, and that your sales levels are high enough to allow your business to be profitable, also take note of where your product or service stands compared to your competition. However do not let the comparison dominate your decision.

Sooner or later, every salon owner deals with the need to raise prices. The task should not be taken lightly. The goal of raising prices, of course, is to generate additional revenue from those accepting the price increase. This should exceed losses from client attrition from those who don't.

If your strategy is poor, the net result could be reduced revenues, fewer clients and perhaps loss of good will, even among those clients who remain. Dreadful on all counts.

Due to this, most pricing consultants, strongly recommend testing the impact of a price increase. Others advise trying the increase in some segments of your price list, before adopting an overall price rise.

Fortunately, most clients are a bit 'sticky.' There are social and emotional connections associated with changing stylists. once again the issue of value will override the price.

Research indicates that while price always matters, it rarely is the only thing that matters, unless you are a discount business. So if the price increase is correctly executed, revenues and profits should be expected to increase.

A recent report concluded that pricing correctly is the fastest and most effective way to increase profits. They found a 1% price rise, if volumes remained stable, could generate an 8% increase in operating profit. A 1% decrease in price or not raising your prices reduces operating profits by 8%. This might seem quite obvious, what it means is that 80% of the price increase will be returned as profit.

USING A COMBINATION OF TACTICS

Just recently I had a consultation with a client, that just purchased a salon from her previous boss. There was no pricing strategy in this business at all. After I had a discussed the situation I devised the following pricing strategy, it included a combination of many pricing strategies.

The eight tactics we used in this strategy were a combination of

1) Cost Plus Margin Pricing

2) Client Education

3) Creating increasing awareness of value

4) Service bundling / package

5) Introducing new products

6) Lowering appointment cost by introducing lower skilled staff for less important tasks ie shampoo, rinse and drying

7) Increasing bundle prices one component at a time

8) Focus marketing on Perceived Value after researching the target market.

After first calculating her cost plus margin target we got her on the road to taking control of her price structure. Bear in mind that there wasn't even an advertised price list when she took over the salon.

After re-pricing her services we created a Price List that Clients could understand. Firstly, we asked her to advertise her Blowdry price. The Blowdry price had never been advertised before and none of her staff even knew the breakdown was somewhere between $20 and $40, we advertised the blowdry as $40 / Plus $20 for Long Hair. This is a substantial price increase but we developed a package that delivered better value for her clients.

We introduced a service 'Scalp Massage $20' the massage would become part of the haircut prewash for the $40 Blowdry, at no extra cost, and only took five Minutes, so no extra seat time.

Her haircuts were to be advertised at $40. If Clients had a Cut and Blowdry it only cost them $70 an increase of $10 (current price $60). However for their $70 they received. A haircut $40 + a Blowdry $40 + Scalp Massage $20, the Total value $100.

The Advertised Package Price $70. The Package Savings $30, all that for only $10 more than they are currently paying.

At no point did mentioned $10 more or the old price $60 (circa). We only advertised what's in the package for ($70), and the clients $30 saving.

To market this the salon owner asked clients, Why do you need this package?

The staffs answer. To cut hair professionally, we need to cut the exterior on damp hair, dry it, then personalise and texturise the interior of the cut before finishing the style. We have designed this package so that we can offer our clients a professional haircut at an affordable price.

The appointment took 45 minutes and looked like this

5 Minute consultation / Senior Stylist

10 minute Wash and Massage / Junior

10 minutes Exterior cut / Senior Stylist

10 minutes Start Blowdry / Junior

10 minutes Personalise Cut, finish Dry and Style / Senior Stylist

In this way the stylist is able to Book two clients and overlap their two appointments. Both would be out in an hour. The second client would be started 10-15 minutes after the first.

The Stylist can generate $93 for the hour against the old $70, their seat time target is only $80. If a little more downtime was factored in for late starts or running over time, this package will still be on target for increased Profit .

In the mean time the salon manager researched every competitor that she aspired to. Those close to hers, and those in Larger towns. She then listed all the things that the others offered, that she Didn't. She selected the things that might matter to her clients and then implemented them into her salon and moved the prices upward accordingly.

The first step in the strategy is to let the clients see the full individual price and realise that they are receiving a sizeable discount for the professional service in the package.

The strategy is, every six months increase the price of one of the components in each package, gradually as more clients take on the package the business will become more efficient and profitable.

ATTRACTIVE PRICING TACTICS

Focus the price increases where they will actually do some good. A small % change in a high price item may produce a bigger result than a larger % change on many lower price items or visa versa.

Assuming that your cost + margin price is lower than your actual advertised price, examine prices charged for the same services among your competitors. You are trying to discover and then focus on price changes among services that are not pulling their weight. You are hoping to increase your prices on these services even more than you have anticipated.

In mature markets, it may be a better strategy to focus on share of wallet rather than share of market. The intent is to capture more sales from current clients rather than a focus on attracting new ones. This use of the pricing tool, will less likely invoke a significant competitive response.

Analyse your sales tickets to determine what the actual 'in the till price' is, as in 'money actually in the till.' Every salon offers a list price, followed by a series of margin reductions, e.g., pensioner discounts, package / volume discount, discount to meet competition, discount for loyalty, redone services, promotion discounts etc. After all the discounts have been applied, the net price is the money in the till price, something far removed from the listed price. If these sources of leakage can be eliminated or reduced, revenues will increase even though the list price does not change.

Not raising all prices of your prices by the same amount can be productive. Prices for key services are closely watched, but not those less used. So, keep the price increase most modest for the key services and raise it more for those less studied.

Add a higher priced option to your packages even though it will likely sell poorly. Most buyers like to be somewhere in the middle of the price/quality distribution. Quite a few never buy the most expensive of anything, thinking it is just not smart. And many never buy the cheapest either, thinking it could be poor quality. By adding a new 'most expensive' option, the new distribution of sales will shift to include greater sales of the formerly most expensive option.

Bundle the sale with extras or premiums. The intent is to add enough perceived value via the premium ,that after the incremental costs of the offer are deducted, net cash from sales is increased, and the current product is no longer comparable with competitor products based on price. Your clients are no longer comparing apples to apples.

Itemise the components of your bundle. This tactic is designed to increase a product's perceived value. It's accomplished by publishing an imputed price for each element of the package even though they will never be sold separately. This should increase the perceived value of the whole and make raising its price easier.

Shrink the offering. This is not really relevant in the hair & beauty industry, except in the case of subscriptions and memberships. The classic method is to keep the price the same, but reduce the inclusions length of the offer, typically it's used in product size and volume of the contents, e.g., putting 150ml of candy in the bag instead of 160ml. The price increase/ volume reduction may not be noticed since labels are not well read. This has been done repeatedly in the food industry, yogurt, candy, coffee, chips. Related is reducing the product's physical size, e.g., newspaper and magazine pages are smaller, 2 x 4s aren't 4 inches wide. Similarly, magazine subscription lengths have been reduced; auto lease mileage allowances have declined, etc.

Increasing the quantity in the package. This is not so farfetched as it seems. If the cost of the packaging is significant, selling one package with twice as much in it, for example, can save money over selling the same amount in two packages. (And it will save inventory handling costs, picking and packing costs, etc.)

How Best to Communicate a Price Increase

If you intend to raise prices, it is imperative to communicate the increase to clients in a timely, appropriate manner. Some price rises require little or no communication with the client.

Several sources argue that a well-presented explanation of the increase, along with specific evidence regarding why it is necessary, will be positively accepted. For example, 'This is being reluctantly done because our Professional product and wage expenses have increased an average of 20% in the past six months, we can no longer absorb this cost increase by ourselves.'

Don't say, 'Product costs and wages expenses have gone up about 20%.'

Research indicates that clients think prices based on costs are 'fair.' This approach makes sense, because often clients will be seeing their costs increase as well, and they may be grappling with the same problem with their clients. Another expert also suggests that government regulations requiring price changes are always a palatable explanation. And it doesn't hurt to remind clients how long it has been since your last increase and how competitive your prices will remain. Here are some guidelines to consider when communicating a price increase:

The client must <u>not</u> think the price increase is being initiated solely to increase profits, i.e., padding profit at their expense. Don't buy a new car, plaster the photos all over facebook, then increase the salon prices the next month.

In addition it is imperative large increases be announced well in advance (at least 30 days), of the time that it goes into effect. This offers clients the last chance to purchase at the old prices. As a practical matter, this may lead to forward buying so be prepared for a bump in near term sales that is likely not to be repeated. There are also staff level and inventory considerations as well. The announcement of an 8% price increase on a major product line or service shouldn't come unexpectedly, out of the blue. Nobody likes to receive price increases, and even worse, nobody likes to receive them without any indication that they are coming. That is why it is better to have regular small increases rather than one annual large increase.

Your best spending clients should receive personal (scripted) communication about the price increase and reasons why it needs to be implemented.

Email and text message blasts are specifically advised against because they seem impersonal and provide less security.

The tone of the message should be one of confidence and matter-of-factness. For example, we take your business and the services we provide very seriously.Unfortunately, Price changes are part of business. "To maintain our current professional service level, we believe our price rise is quite justified."

While, what to say is clear, there is no common advice regarding how best to say it. This may be an opportunity to solidify your company's Brand Personality via creative copy, design, etc. Remember, this is another important touch-point with clients.

However there is one proviso; Unless you are clearly offering additional value, the price increase must not place you so out of relative position vs. competition, that clients are encouraged to look elsewhere. This requires a competitor price check, e.g., look at their websites, check with your stylists, ask clients who are 'friends' of your salon. Weight this up against your Perceived value Price and/or Cost + margin calculation. Your competitor price check should only be a guide and shouldn't dominate your decision.

TAKE THE INITIATIVE AND OFFER ALTERNATIVES.

If you sense that the price increase is going to prompt the client to search for an alternative, take the initiative and offer an alternative. Do a little research. If your salon purchases high priced products, and they are going up by 6%, as you tell your clients the details of the price increase, suggest that they may want to consider a less expensive alternative. Have the alternative service or product ready to discuss with the client.

This does a number of things. Firstly, it communicates to the client that the price increase is a done deal, the only option is to buy a product of lesser quality. There is no option to beat down the price increase. In this way you get the client thinking of alternatives.

Secondly, it allows you to decipher the mind of the client. When given the option of considering a less expensive alternative, if the client shows no interest in the option, it's a good indication that he's going to accept the price increase, and not shop around.

Thirdly, if the client bites on the less expensive alternative, then you are still in the game. It's better to retain the client with a less expensive alternative, and maybe lose a little sales volume or gross margin dollars, then it is to lose the client, and walk away with nothing.

Take the initiative, use some of the Tactics that we have previously spoken about. **Raise prices as you add services**. If all you do is raise your price, your clients will naturally focus solely on that price increase. But if you have new services or products ready to roll out, it's fairly easy to lessen the impact of a price increase.

The key, is to show greater value along with higher prices. While some clients focus on price alone, most consider the balance of value and price. Show you are offering greater value, and the price increase may become insignificant.

You don't always have to raise prices in order to increase margins. Lowering volume while maintaining the same price automatically increases your profit margin. If a restaurant can often decrease portions while maintaining price, salons can do a similar thing. Introduce a cool new shampoo range that oh, by the way holds 100ml of shampoo instead of 125ml will naturally increase your margins.

Sometimes the best way to 'raise' prices is to cut costs. While decreasing fixed costs is certainly possible, in the short term the easiest and quickest payback comes from attacking variable costs.

Focus on areas like service time, labor, productivity and quality control. And while you're at it, attack semi-variable areas like maintenance and utility costs. Reduce any expense and your bottom line will automatically improve without raising prices.

You could use cost saving measures with your professional stock like weighing colour mixes, and having measured pourers for basin stock.

Don't forget packages, we have discussed this in length earlier, Clients tend to assume they get a better deal when products or services are bundled, even when they can't determine the cost of individual items. Create a bundle of similar services, or create a bundle of products with a complementary service, and you may be able to raise prices on some of the individual items while masking that increase inside the bundle.

Off peak pricing, is another way to take the initiative. You could charge more for services at peak times i.e. Saturday Morning, Thursday evening etc, Raise your prices then offer a discount at off peak times. Again, provide additional value at a higher price and most clients will be less resistant to the change. In fact, some may willingly switch to the options.

BE CONFIDENT AND MATTER OF FACT AND EXPLAIN.

Price increases are a fact of life at certain points in the economic cycle. Nobody likes them, but no one client can stem the tide. So, your client has to adjust to the fact of rising prices, just like you and your suppliers do.

Understand you must be confident. If you are tentative, timid and intimidated by the price increase, you'll stimulate lots of push back from the client. That push back is doomed to take up a lot of your time, and the client's time. You'd both be better off just accepting the fact of life that prices are going up. Adjust, and go on with your business.

That should be your attitude. Convey it in your demeanour, in your attitude and in your conversation. Be confident and your client will likely react in a similar manner towards you.

In some cases, you may have no option but to simply raise prices, when you are forced to raise prices due to a dramatic impact on costs. If you retail products and the cost of those products has increased by double-digit percentages, your clients will understand if you are forced to raise prices in order to stay in business. If that happens industry wide, let your clients know why you'll need to raise prices.

Most are already aware of the situation and will understand. They won't love it, but they will understand.

BENCHMARKS

To plot business progress we need to use, set or create benchmarks for key income generating services and key growth monitors otherwise known as K.P.I.

These benchmarks allow us to plan our future growth and assist with client satisfaction, keeping our business focused on the key indicators for maximising our business profit. To maintain enthusiasm and motivation, these benchmarks are also used to monitor the teams performance and productivity, hopefully allowing us to pay our team members a percentage of the increased profits.

In the following chapters, I'm going to discuss benchmarks for our business and team, followed by how to setup effective and easily understood bonus or Commission Systems.

At this point we have discussed and hopefully understand how to calculate our prices using a blend of cost plus margin pricing and perceived value pricing, doing this has also incorporated many aspects of customer care.

Because we have based our perceived value pricing on the specific services and value that our target clients seek, we have been able to create a strong client base, that allows our business to increase profit, as well as increase our client numbers at a steady pace. The next goal is to improve and maintain our profit levels, to achieve this, we must improve our productivity and continually increase our client base.

A Client base increase will occur naturally, if we continue to provide our specific client model with the service that they value, that is providing the look, feel and skill level within our business. Skill level would also include moving with current fashion and new technology that applies to our target client model.

Benchmarking is an interesting topic, in general benchmarking is confused with "comparison". An inexperienced manager would seek out industry benchmarks, and statistics of average salon results and **compare** these results to the performance of the salon.

Thats nice enough, and interesting, if you hope to discover that your performance is above average. You might also gain some insight into some benchmarks that you could use as a guide for your salon. If you are well outside these industry comparisons it is a good idea to ask your self why?

The truth is, a comparison is not a benchmark. Benchmarks are markers that an experienced manager would set, in order to monitor performance, with a particular focus on areas deemed important to the increased profitability of the business.

The first step would be to discuss and agree on specific services or procedures of importance in your business, where you could monitor, and plan improvement.

A benchmark will not necessarily give you an immediate insight into individual or team performance, client satisfaction or growth in any specific area of your business. A benchmark can however indicate changes in behaviour. Your job, is to dig deep and find out what is causing these changes. Benchmarks need to be specific to **your** business, if you are making a profit you need to be monitoring the profitable areas in your business, so you can keep them that way. You should be able to easily monitor growth in all the important areas. Comparisons are generally not specific and often not relevant.

The trouble with benchmarking arrives, when we try to compare our individual benchmarks, to those supplied by the industry. Not that the Industry supplied benchmarks are incorrect, it is that they are generally an average result from across the industry, or a broad range that offers no specifics. This often means that they are dangerously irrelevant to your business. Many tend to use the number of staff as the common bond. This is not necessarily accurate, a low end "sweaty betty", with cheap prices with 4 staff is not comparable to a high priced Colour Specialist with 4 staff.

Benchmarks need to be specific to your business. Even though you might decide to use the same benchmarks as other Businesses. Your target, and the results between your needs and theirs will vary greatly, meaning that direct comparison using industry averages, could steer you away from a profitable result.

There is also the problem of miscalculating or misinterpreting the statistics, here is an example. An often quoted statistic is that your wages should be approximately 40% of your expenses, some salon owners misinterpret this as 40% of their actual income, or maybe 40% of the income target. In this instance, the misuse of income instead of expenses as the benchmark, would have a variation in our target of somewhere between 20 and 30%. This is an enormous variation. This example highlights only one the dangers in direct comparison from one business to another.

Here are some broad ranges that the Australian Tax Office recommends for salons, note in the first graph the labour wage to turnover ratio is a massive 24%-44%. Almost invariably this does not include all of the Owners Wages. This benchmark is not a true reflection of salon operations it is a true reflection of what owners claim to be happening.

Benchmark Range	$50,000 to $150,000	$150,001 to $300,000	More than $300,000
Labour/turnover	24% - 37%	28% - 39%	34% – 44%
Rent/turnover	15% – 22%	11% – 16%	9% – 15%
Motor vehicle expenses/ turnover	3% – 4%	1% – 2%	1%

TAX RETURNS	$50,000 to $150,000	$150,001 to $300,000	More than $300,000
Cost of sales/turnover	12% – 17%	12% – 17%	13% – 17%
Average cost of sales	15%	15%	15%
Total expenses/turnover	52% – 68%	70% – 83%	79% – 88%
Average total expenses	60%	77%	84%

BAS Statement	$50,000 to $150,000	$150,001 to $300,000	More than $300,000
Non-capital purchases/ total sales	39% – 51%	37% – 46%	36% – 45%

I'm going to list some of the benchmarks that are commonly or not commonly used in the hair & beauty industry. I'm not saying that you should use any of these benchmarks, this simply a list. I will explain and debunk some these benchmarks as we go on. You should choose a benchmark that is easy to monitor and easily understood by your staff and management, most importantly the benchmark should be used to increase your Gross income.

MONITORING CLIENT NUMBERS

1). Monitor the Number of new clients, and the number of non returning clients. This one of my favourite set of statistics. I believe this is an excellent starting point. When you find an anomaly and delve a little deeper, this becomes a great way to measure the effectiveness of your marketing, also of the quality of service and skill of your operators. It is also a way to view how well you are delivering the value your target market is seeking. I like this benchmark, because it allows you to ask targeted questions. Most salon's have a consistent number of new clients visiting their salon each week, it could be six, or 10, maybe even 20 depending on the size of the salon, the number doesn't matter, so don't compare it to someone else. What does matter is, that the number is growing or at worst static!

If you then measure the number of clients that you are servicing each week you can start your comparison. Over the years I have found, that despite new client arriving each week, the overall number of clients per week remains the same.

If this is the case, you should research what type of client is not returning, or what services these clients not rebooking for, or to which staff member these clients not returning.

This comparison will give you an insight as to whether you need to Focus your marketing and a service offer to a particular client demographic, or whether you need education in the delivery of a particular service, or for particular staff members. Even if this was the only benchmark that you measured, you would be effectively using your benchmark to improve your business. A variation on this that will allow even closer inspection is, to divide the number of clients that each team member services into the number of hours each has worked. The result is clients per hour, now you can directly compare each staff member. The example below allows you to ask the questions:

- How many Clients per hour do I need to make a profit?
- Is this benchmark achievable?
- If not, what must I improve to achieve the benchmark?
- Why are some team member not marking the benchmark?
- Is the reason, Price, Skill, Attitude?

	Hours worked	Clients / week	Clients / Hour
Kathy	38	28	0.7
Jess	26	22	0.8
Kylie	26	10	0.4
Charli	40	36	0.9

I have used this example, to demonstrate that with a simple internal benchmark, you can target issues within your own business and focus on improvement. It doesn't matter what any one else is doing. Simply focus on your own improvement.

You can apply the same logic to how many new clients are visiting your business, focusing on how many per month, and the ask the similar questions of your performance.

2). Income, this is the most commonly used benchmark, probably because it is the easiest one to monitor. Monetary targets are easy for your staff to understand, but I do believe that's service income and retail income should be separated and it addressed individually. This is the perfect benchmark **not** to compare. I have worked with Individual salons whose income, varied between $3000 and $90,000 per week. When you're using income as a benchmark it must be purely internal. You should look at individual team members income growth, often with a salon, it is often non-specific, to compare one individuals income with another, as there are many variables. For example, the day or shift that someone works, the length of service at the salon, experience and education. What is important is, the income is increasing, and above the salons hourly needs. My verdict is, if you use income as a benchmark it should not be the primary benchmark used to determine profitability or performance.

3).Average Client bill is another income benchmark commonly used, *(difficult to use effectively)*. This was used extensively as an ego trip for some salon owners twenty years ago, it was used like a, how good are we boast. I believe that it is a totally non comparable statistic. It does little to help you predict crucial changes in client or staff behaviour, it can only indicate that there may be changes. If you decide to use this, choose a more specific data set for your benchmark eg, average client bill from chemical services per client each week.

4). Three times your wage. *(do not use this)* This is a benchmark based on the cost of wages?!? Not clients needs, not overall expenses, not based on the profit you need. This is not based on any sane formula. *3 times your wage is not a benchmark, target, or comparison, it was an observation, it is not a benchmark for individual performance or profitability.*

In general, salon owners decide on monetary targets by simply pulling a figure out of a hat. They guess an amount they think is fair, based on what they guess they need to earn. More often than not, it's based on the legendary three times your wage theory. I have 3 staff each net wage is $1000 per week therefore I need $9000 per week, or was it gross wage? This sort of benchmarking is simply, a wild <u>un</u>educated guess.

While I am here, I might as well explain to you where this calculation came from. In the 1950s in Sydney, a well respected salon owner made the observation, that if his staff could generate three times their wage he would be able to make a profit. I had the pleasure of meeting him in the early 1990's. This was definitely was an accurate observation for <u>his</u> salon.

It may have been a workable figure in the 1950's when there was no GST or superannuation, low insurance and low or no workers compensation fees. I'm also not sure whether he owned his building, in fact, I have no idea what his costs plus margin price needed to be, nor does anyone else know his seat time needs. This being the case, only a fool would blindly use this

70-year-old observation as a benchmark to guide their profitability in today's competitive and saturated market.

I can hear it now, usually, after I have pointed these facts out in a presentation, someone idiot will, yell out, oh yes, I use 3.5 Times their wage or four times their wage, in the belief, that by plucking another imaginary figure from their mind they will appear intelligent. Only when you have accurately calculated your Seat time, you can accurately set benchmarks for your staff and your business. Please never use legendary, mythical or imaginary calculations to plan your business future, even if they were an accurate observation 70 years ago.

Simple, sensible calculations that focus on core elements of your business, must be used to create benchmarks that you can easily monitor. It is that Simple.

Here is a beauty, (NOT). At recent presentation, someone in the audience asked if I could comment on the calculation that her "business coach" (gypsy), told her she should use as method of calculating a weekly target for her staff, from that point she would be able to calculate what she needed each week.

The formula went something like this. Add up all your expenses divide them by 52, and multiply them by four, then divide them the number of hours the salon is open, then add 20% for your retail target, then multiply that by the number of staff. You then have the weekly target for a 38 hour employee. Obviously there is no logic to this, this is simply hocus pocus. After I picked myself up off the floor I answered with wry smile,

"I'm going to suggest you find another snake oil salesman".

My objection to simply creating a monetary target is that there is no consideration for your clients. Which buy the way, should be your only consideration. There can be no culture of customer care, if your staff are simply focused on money.

If you study what your clients value, then create benchmarks that drive your business to these goals, you are not only focusing your staff on your clients needs, but you will be able to monetise these benchmarks, then you can set parameters that your staff can easily strive towards.

5). Unit Sales.*(this can be perfect)* Units sales as a target, is an interesting and effective concept, you could simply state that a team member needs to do 10 colours per week or sell 10 retail units per week. A more specific way to do this would be to suggest that each team member needs to sell six colours for every 10 clients or six retail units for every 10 clients. How you do this, is by monetising the benchmark, for example, if a stylist does 30 clients a week and your target is six colour service units per 10 clients, she would need to do 18 colour units. If the profit on each colour service unit is $70 then the weekly profit *(not income)* for colour would it be $1260 per stylist. Unit sales targeting is another of my favourite ways to benchmark. It has many positive aspects if done correctly. You need to choose what units are specific to your target demographic. You also need to monetise these service unit accurately. If you do this, you don't need to worry about individual income, You simply have to measure how many units per 10 clients, then drive your team forward by focusing on your appointment and how to sell these units. This type of measurement is also easy for your team to understand and is a fair measure of productivity as it is based on the number of clients serviced each week.

We can, and should, set benchmarks to improve productivity effectively, in less tangible ways, like focusing on rebooking current clients or downtime hours. By reducing the time between visits we increase the number of services over a period, thereby effectively increasing the number of clients we service, without actually increasing the number of individuals. Focus your team's attention toward rebooking high ticket value services, typically cut and colour clients. The higher ticket value allows you to offer rewards to your clients for rebooking. Loss leader promotions are particularly good in this instance, this is where you can introduce clients to new products or services.

An example of a loss leader promotion would it be, to offer a retail product to your client for a price that is slightly above your cost, let's say any shampoo or conditioner for $18 instead of the usual retail price of $45. The client would purchase the product on their next visit, provided they rebook today within a 4 to 6 week timeframe, and providing they honour the booking. In this instance the client feels that they are getting a $45 product for only $18, you might only make 1 or $2 profit on the product yourself, but your client believes that they have been given a $27 discount. In their eyes they received a discount for making the rebooking not for a reduced value service. Your business on the other hand has sold, a $200 plus service, an $18 dollar product and secured the same booking in 4 to 6 weeks time. I have in some salons implemented this, and sold it as a $5 product not $18, I have actually seen the best results at $5.

Achieving good results from rebooking could lead to requiring more staff at your busiest times, so a management focus on the staff roster is important at this stage.

6). Using Downtime as a benchmark, is an effective way to improve productivity. The interesting thing about downtime is, we have already factored it into our price, as a downtime allowance. If we can effectively reduce our current downtime the majority of the income from this will be profit, this will push our hourly income upward and effectively create a price rise without moving up prices upward.

The typical Salon I have dealt with over the last 15 years has had a downtime range of between 25 and 35%. It is very rare for a salon to have less than 20% downtime. Downtime isn't such a bad thing particularly if you can add the downtime cost back into your prices. In fact if you have less than 20% downtime you need to sharpen your management skills, more than likely you're extremely busy at the most popular times and possibly need more staff than you currently have during those busy periods.

Let's have a deeper look and dissect 20% down time. 20% down time for an employee over a 40 hour week, is only eight hours per week, that's eight hours over five days. That means on Tuesday, Wednesday & Thursday only two hours per day with no clients, then on Friday & Saturday only 1 hour with no clients.

If this example applied to every one of your employees you would have 20% Downtime across your salon. If your team has less downtime than that example you need to employ some more staff.

7). Clients per hour: This, is not the same as, but is calculated in the table, in point 1). Clients per hour is simple a starting point, but a good example of setting a simple benchmark, that all can understand, also specific to the individual business. A client of mine used this very successfully, I didn't really recommend this one, but he had a second phase of measurement to help grow his business, that's the reason it was a successful strategy. Initially he calculated that, if a staff member could do 4 clients every 5 hours they would generate a profit (that's 32 clients in 40 hours). I know there are many variables, for example, if the staff member did 4 cut & dry, compared to 4 Colour services etc. But in his model, he only advertised and specialised in Cut & Colour Packages. His theory was that it was his job to promote colour, and that promotion would drive more colour services to the clients that entered the salon. In this instance his staff would automatically have a high cut & colour representation in their clients numbers. Apart from client numbers, his second phase of deliberation, was surveying his clients and monitoring the percentage of colours each stylists did, this gave him an insight into the skill of each team member. In his business, he made a success of using this simple benchmark to grow his business, thats all he needed to do.

INDUSTRY BENCHMARKS

Average is Average, you don't want to be Average.

There have been some inroads made, and some hard work done by members of the hairdressing community, to collate information that can help salon owners to measure the performance of their salon. In fact, there are benchmarking companies outputting a great deal of data, that will allow you to compare yourself with industry averages. By looking at these Benchmarks and results, you may be able choose some parameters that suit your business. Remember what I've said earlier, these figures are great to look at and compare, as a ball park guide, but don't neck yourself if you are outside the average. Choose some of the K.P.I's to benchmark, monitor your performance and create internal growth in the chosen, specific areas of your business. Compare your Growth to yourself, not the other salons. You only need growth.

Members of the hairdressing industry, are notoriously poor performers, when it comes to consistency. Their consistency is poor in relation to skill, caring for clients, following directions from the salon management and the worst of all sales. By Sales I mean up-selling of services, home care and home maintenance.

I believe there are three key components needed to operate a profitable salon. Focus your team on:

- **Chemical services**
- **Rebooking your clients**
- **Retail sales**

If you have consistently high results in those three areas you'll will be running a profitable business.

Skill level, and an education culture within the salon is a core component for achieving your benchmarks. There is an assumption that a hairdressers skill is at a reasonably high baseline, this is almost universally not the case. A moderate skill level, and a poor education culture in the fashion industry will undermined your teams ability to reach any of your benchmarks, due to fact that fashion and the required skills are constantly changing.

Your entire team must be able to move with change, and have a high level of competency. There is no room for team members, who do not engage in education every single year. Especially those who have been in the industry for many years. These employees are most often the ones that have been left behind when it comes to fashion and new techniques. These team members often dampen the enthusiasm, the knowledge and growth aspects of your business because they don't want to attend, or don't want to pay for external education. They also dissuade other team members, because they fear dropping down the pecking order as others become more advanced in their skills.

Obviously, the ultimate goal for the business is an increase in gross profit, however when you analyse the income from the three key components you will be able to monetise the result then set a benchmark from each, to meets your monetary targets.

Let's take a look at some of the industry standards and the necessary benchmarks for these three key components

CHEMICAL SERVICES

Industry avg=2.5 chemical services for every 10 clients
Min. Expect performance = 6 in 10
Excellent Performance = 7-9 Chemical Clients for every 10

Chemical Services are amongst the most lucrative services for a salon business. The Industry average for the number of clients having chemical services for every 10 clients is 2.5.

Salon owners, generally average eight or more Chemical service clients for every 10. There is a major discrepancy between Number of chemical service clients done by an employee when compared it to the salon owner. And experienced senior stylist should average at least six Chemical service clients in 10.

If we base income from a chemical service on a cut and colour package that sold for $200, and assumed that a 40 hour per week employee would service 36 clients, the gross income from 2.5 cut and colour clients in ten will be, $1800 per week. The gross income for 6 services In 10 would be $4320 per week. I'll say no more.

RETAIL SALES

Industry average =2 units in 10
Min. Expect performance = 6
Excellent Performance = 7-9 Retail Units for every 10 clients

Recommending and selling retail products in my mind is Money for Jam, you outlay for non-perishable stock that takes up very little floor space, your profit is between 30 & 50% of the gross sale, in a beauty salon these necessary sales, should be up to 50% of your gross income.

Sadly, your staff don't take retailing seriously, after all "they are hairdressers not salespeople"? (vomit). Retail sales are really home care, your team will need education, even if retail income is only a small component of your gross turnover, that doesn't mean it's not worth the effort. Home care breeds client loyalty, remember the survey stating, clients change salons because they feel they are not cared about. Discussing home care means you care. Even if your profit isn't that great, It's the person care that your clients want.

The Industry average for the number of retail units sold for every 10 clients is only 2. That's retail units not the number of clients that purchase.

Salon owners again average higher than their employees at six units to 10 clients, six in 10 is still an achievable Target, especially if good systems and rewards are in place.

If we base income from a retail Product at $35, and assumed that a 40 hour per week employee would service 36 clients, the income from 2 retail units in ten will be, $252 per week. 6 In 10 would be $756 per week.

REBOOKING KEY CLIENTS

Rebooking your clients is seriously underestimated, probably because putting a monetary figure on is quite difficult, also the weekly growth becomes exponential.

Let's put this simply, suppose I'm rebooking at the industry average of 3 clients for every 10. That means during each of my first five weeks I would Book 10 clients out 36 on into a five week cycle. The next five weeks I rebook six different clients on a five week cycle, in the following five weeks I rebook another six clients on a five weeks cycle, in just 15 weeks I'll have 22 clients re-booking each week on a five week cycle, that's over 6 in ten.

Why is it that in nearly every salon stylists operate at three rebooking in 10, but their client numbers remain the same? The answer is they are not actually doing any rebooking, three rebookings a week can be achieved without even mentioning the word rebook. In reality if I got three extra clients to rebook each week I'd be rebooking 8 in10 clients, within a year I would be fully booked out.

The truth is your team doesn't care about rebooking, because they're bloody lazy, because they want to do things "their way". While recently consulting, I had a team member tell me that's she wasn't going to ask her clients to rebook because, they would come back when they wanted to, not when the salon told them to. Unfortunately that stylist became financially unviable and she's doing things "her way", somewhere else. It is a shame, but as a salon owner you can't Legally Express the truth, for fear of causing, "anxiety" or "depression" or heaven forbid you might be accused of "Bullying" or "trying to make a Profit". Don't get me started.

Don't "despair", you can develop a really good rebooking culture in your salon with some manipulation, and make it easy for your staff to rebook clients. The upshot of rebooking is, that not only do your clients visit your salon between 3 & 5 times more each year, there is also the potential for additional services and retail sales. A good rule of thumb for booking cut

& colour clients is four weeks for short hair, five weeks four medium length hair and six weeks for long hair.

The Industry average for the number of rebookings in every 10 clients is only 3. Salon owners again average higher than their employees at six or more rebookings to 10 clients.

In the following example we will assume the same as earlier, that income from a cut and colour service is $200, a 40 hour per week employee would service 36 clients, and the average rebooked client is moving from 8 weeks to a 5 week cycle.

In this case, each client would visit the salon an extra 3.9 times each year. The additional weekly income at 6 rebookings in ten will be, $324 per week per stylist.

Apart from providing your clients the services that they value and concentrating on the skills needed to grow your business. The monetary effects of focusing on benchmarks for our 3 key components are:

Chemical service figures increased by, $2520 per week per stylist. Retail sales figures increased by, $504 per week per stylist. Increased income from Rebooking was a minimum of $243 per week per stylist.

This represents a total INCREASE in income of, $3267 per week, per 40 hour stylist, or $81.68 per hour per stylist. This figure is not what each stylist made <u>it is what they increased their income by</u>.

Sharing this across you team. If your team currently has the average sales results and you have 3 seniors and part-timer, that's 140 productive hours each week, by reaching 6 in 10, your salon income would **increase** by $11,434 each week.

Increased weekly income per stylist

	Industry Avg income / week	6 units in 10 Income / week
Chemical Services	$1800.00	$4320.00
Retail Unit Sales	$252.00	$756.00
Rebooking	$81.00	$324.00
Weekly income	$2133.00	$5400.00
ADDITIONAL WEEKLY INCOME PER STYLIST		**$3267.00**

Apply these three benchmarks to your salon, and you'll realise how much additional income your team can generate if they reached these simple benchmarks. Better still you can motivate them to greater success, by giving them a percentage of the income above this target.

Of course, you could set other benchmarks and I'm sure there are many businesses in the industry that require different benchmarks, if you're operating a barbershop or a beauty salon for example. It doesn't matter what your business is, the theory is the same, look for a benchmark that reflects the services your clients value, then focus on that benchmark. This is the starting point at which you should reward your staff, their reward should be a portion of everything above this benchmark.

BONUSES & COMMISSIONS

Before we start, Commissions are different to Bonuses, so let's get our terminology in tune. When I say commission I mean, we pay a percentage of turnover or a specific sale, there may also be a retainer or a minimum target, an example would be, each time your sales person sells a particular product or service you will pay that person a percentage of the income.

A commission is pretty straightforward. You may be introducing a new service or a new product, to drive additional sales you give your team a Percentage each time they sell one to a client. Commissions are normally paid in situations where the commission is an essential part of the employees wage.

A commission on gross sales, is not always a great idea in a salon situation, as doesn't normally contain a qualifying target, everyone gets a slice of the gross turnover, thereby having the potential to reduce your income before you have covered your expenses. A Commission is best paid on retail product sales, and may or may not require the inclusion of a qualifying target.

Bonuses get a little more complicated, in general bonuses are paid when someone on a wage or salary does something above and beyond what they are paid for. In the employees eyes the reward is not necessarily linked to a percentage of turn over, it is more likely perceived as a flat payment or gift.

For a bonus system to be sustainable, you need a total mind shift form the norm. You should only develop a Bonus system to increase profit, not to boost your staffs weekly wage. When you make additional Profit above your overall target, you reward them with a portion. If you set your bonus system only to increase your staffs weekly wage you will end up simply giving away money and eating into your current profit.

A simple, but poorly thought out bonus system (**do not use)** would go something like this: Your teams benchmark is, 3 times their wage, and you offer to pay $100 to anyone that reaches their target. The problem arises when the second, third and fourth employees do not reach their target, this means you are giving away money and you haven't even reached your minimum income target.

The next problem to arise will be, what is three times your wage? Your employees will start questioning, is three times a wage Gross Wage, or is it take home wage, does it include super? Do you deduct GST from the total? What happens when they work overtime? The list goes on and on, but I can assure you, those that do not reach the target will question the target, every single time, your target cannot be ambiguous. Please **do not use** this example, I have actually worked with a salon that used this as their bonus system. I can describe it in one word "disaster". The example is far too simple to be effective in the complex social atmosphere residing in a modern hairdressing salon. Each Month the team would calculate their bonus and each month the calculation was different, no one actually ever received a bonus.

When you introduce a bonus system into your team culture, there are many aspects you must consider. Initially your Bonus system must be fair and agreed upon by all.

From the employee point of view: PERFORMANCE related bonus systems are positively associated with job satisfaction, and trust in management. PROFIT related Bonus Systems do not have similar positive effects, in fact, profit related pay results in employees being less committed and less trusting of management. This is a real dilemma because you can only offer a bonus system based on profit. A point that is often misunderstood by an employee.

Employees prefer targets, like the number of cuts, or the number of colours, rather than how much money they generated. However, they also said that a bonus system needs to be fair, accessible to all team members, easy to understand, achievable, and most importantly you must not change the rules, unless you have the agreement of all parties, which, after implementation is nearly impossible. The worst thing you can do is to create a bonus System to appease disgruntled employees. Promising a reward to someone who is unmotivated is a bit like offering salt water to someone who is thirsty. Bribes in the workplace simply can't work for any length of time.

From the Salon Business point of view: The bonus system must increase profit, therefore making it affordable, dare I say, "sustainable" everything has to be sustainable nowadays. I hate to burst the bubble, but nothing is sustainable, we can only try to make it last a little longer.

Bonus payments, can only be paid from overall salon profit, not when an individual makes his or her target. Your bonus system must drive the team to greater productivity, and it must be easy to administer.

What Should I Reward, Who will I Reward

Bonus and incentive programs can effectively drive employee behaviour and yield the desired business results. However, if not properly designed and implemented, bonus and incentive programs can become a major barrier to business success and create high levels of employee frustration.

There is no single benchmark that can fit the incredible variety of business situations, I've listed are some of the things that you could benchmark and monetise for an employee bonus plan.

- Gross individual service income

- Unit Sales, eg. Retail units, Chemical Services, Rebooking, client numbers.

- Gross Retail Income

- Performance improvement this is especially good system for junior staff making a transition to senior ranks.

- Per Hour Benchmarks such as, Income per hour or Clients per hour.

An excellent bonus structure, that may help decide who to reward will need to contain many of the following elements.

1). A Weekly salon qualifying target that needs to be met before any bonus is paid this is essential in every bonus system, this would normally be a minimum gross income target for the whole salon, or a minimum number of clients per week. Do not include retail income Service income and retail sales should be separate.

2). Individual targets based on the number of hours they work. It should be something easy for the employee to understand like $75 per hour. The most important thing is that the individual targets appear fair to all involved. Hourly targets are great when you have people who work part time, the calculation is simple for you and for your employees.

3). The Bonus should be a percentage of the amount that each individual has made <u>above their target</u>. The percentage should be the same for all. You could add a flat amount eg $100 for achieving the target but only if you have written a provision for bonus amount into your "seat time" price and only if the Salon Qualifying target is met.

4). Your receptionist or front of house should receive a bonus when your minimum weekly qualifying target is reached. They should also receive a percentage of bonuses paid to individuals, particularly if your qualifying target is gross weekly income. Having your receptionist in control of the money coming in is scary enough, however, if you tie gross income to their bonus there maybe less incentive to squirrel away some of that income.

5). Your apprentices or assistants should also be given some thought, they are often incapable of reaching targets that are set in bonus system. However their inclusion and enthusiasm is important in driving qualified stylist towards their bonus. Particularly if the apprentice is going to receive a percentage of any bonus that is paid, even if it only 10% of a senior bonus or a couple of dollars for each retail unit sold by the stylist. Remember retail units are not included in the seat time needs, when paying a retail commission, the profit on each unit sold remains as profit.

HOW MUCH & WHAT TIME FRAME?

This amount is ultimately up to you, some owners pay weekly others monthly, quarterly or major bonuses at the end of the year. I believe that a bonus period should be on a 4 week cycle. The reason I prefer a 4 week cycle is, a 4 week cycle will give exactly 13 cycles each year. The results from each cycle can be directly compared to another on "per client basis", and you can map performance easily.

When choosing an amount to pay be very careful with your calculations, remember the idea of this is to make more profit. Steer away from the trap of offering a set amount of income or a percentage greater than 20%. There are costs to you and to the staff member that need to be drawn from the bonus. I'll use an example to show you how much profit you actually make on amounts above your Target.

Let's assume that your salon this particular week made target. Even though you made that target only one of your senior stylists generated more income than their individual target. The stylist actually made $500 more than their target

On the following table, I've given two examples, 20% then 60% bonus of the profit was paid to the employee. The 20% bonus plus Superannuation equaled $110 for the employee, which will be reduced by income tax, the Salon Profit was $168 after all was taken into account, about a 60 / 40 Split in the salons favour (33%) to the salon. In the second example we offered a 60% of profit bonus, in this case the salon profit was only $14 out of the $500 above target about a 48 / 1 Split, in the Staffs favour (2.8%) to the salon. You can see how easy it is to give away all of your profit.

BONUS PAID AT 60% OF ABOVE TARGET INCOME:

SERVICE BONUS PERCENTAGE =	60
AMOUNT ABOVE TARGET =	$500.00
BONUS PAID	$330.00
SALON PROFIT	$14.00
EXPENSES FOR ABOVE TARGET INCOME	
GST%	10
PRODUCTS & FIXED COST%	5
BONUS PERCENTAGE%	60
10% SUPER ON BONUS	6
COMMISSION FOR RECEPTIONIST %	5
COMMISSION FOR APPRENTICE %	10
EXPENSES SUBTOTAL %	96
PROVISION FOR TAX%	1.2
TOTAL PERCENTAGE FOR EXPENSES	97.2
SALON PROFIT REMAINING %	2.8

Bonus Paid at 20% of Above Target Income:

SERVICE BONUS PERCENTAGE =	20
AMOUNT ABOVE TARGET =	$500.00
BONUS PAID	$110.00
SALON PROFIT	$168.00
EXPENSES FOR ABOVE TARGET INCOME	
GST%	10
PRODUCTS & FIXED COST%	5
BONUS PERCENTAGE%	20
10% SUPER ON BONUS	2
COMMISSION FOR RECEPTIONIST %	5
COMMISSION FOR APPRENTICE %	10
EXPENSES SUBTOTAL %	52
PROVISION FOR TAX%	14.4
TOTAL PERCENTAGE FOR EXPENSES	66.4
SALON PROFIT REMAINING %	33.6

There could be a positive twist, if you've included a $100 provision for bonus in your cost plus margin calculation, it would have been generated this week, you could pay your employee an additional amount, the bonus payment could be $80 for making the target Plus 20% of the profit ($110). This now makes the bonus more attractive to your team member, you will only need to remove the GST and a 10% for superannuation from your $100 bonus provision amount. Returning the employee a total bonus of $190. My suggestion is that 20% is the most you should ever think about, 10% plus a qualifying bonus (set amount) would be fairer. You could set Incremental Benchmarks above the individuals target, for example, if your Salon qualifying target has been met, an individual target might be $3000=$80 bonus, upon reaching $3500 they would receive $80 plus 10% of income between $3000 & $3500, on reaching $4000, would give them 15% of income between $3000 & $4000 and increase to 20% of income when they reached $4500. In this case the employee would stay on the same percentage until they reached the next $500 increment, hopefully driving them towards the next benchmark.

SHOULD I ONLY PAY MONEY?

This is always an interesting debate. As with your clients, your team members will only stay with your business as long as you offer the value that they seek. Money always starts as a motivator but loses its gloss after a while. Your team will be driven by many things, money amongst them. The overriding condition is, the reward must be something in the employee actually wants.

Once you have calculated the amount of money you can spend on the bonus, you can apply it to each individual in different forms, or combination of forms (money plus something) it could be.

- Money payed as wages

- Given as a gift card, or to a store or supplier, even a tab at a restaurant or similar outlet.

- Applied to salon services or products, in this case the actual value all the reward is far greater than the cost to you. A product hamper with a retail value of $400 may only cost you $150 with a little help from your product company.

- Privileges, longer lunch break, afternoon off, late starts.

- Points systems: each dollar and could be classed as one point and you could have a set of rewards that require various numbers of points before they can be redeemed. Which could be used for education or tools and equipment

- Paying for education.

As with perceived value pricing, the value that you put on each reward is the value of that it would cost the employee. For example a $450 dollar pair of scissors could possibly be purchased wholesale for $250, the value to the employee is $450 or 450 points. The same applies to gift cards, you could purchase a $150 dollar restaurant voucher for $125 or less, again the value to the employee is $150 or 150 points.

Offering your team other incentives like education, Time off, holidays, tools and equipment all have their place. Offering your apprentices education rather than money it Is an excellent way to improve your salon profit while keeping your apprentice motivated and developing their skill. Assisting with the purchase of scissors and electrical equipment is another great replacement for money, while making sure the standards in your salon remain high. Allowing time off and paying for holidays / long weekends also is a good substitute for money but should be used sparingly as it reduces it your productive hours therefore your profit margin.

How Will a Bonus System Affect my Business

Your Goal is to produce a structured a bonus system, with achievable benchmarks, that tick all the boxes for your employees. While still producing a steady increased profit for your business. IF you can achieve this your business should thrive.

In a stable work place, everyone actually knows their place, the owner's the boss, the manager is 2IC, you're qualified stylists rank themselves at the top in a social order generally based on their years of experience in the Industry, the apprentices and other team members line up from the tea and tidy person, then first year apprentices upward. If a lower rank suddenly out performs and receives more praise or money than a higher ranked stylist your troubles will begin.

If your bonus structure only rewards individuals, it allows for manipulation of the somewhat stable social structure within the salon. As stylists begin to earn their bonus, jealousy, backstabbing, manipulating the bonus system and division within the team will rear its ugly head.

Most salon owners & managers would agree that motivated, productive stylists are crucial for any business success, regardless of salon size, location, or corporate strategy. The question is how to motivate your team. Offering employees performance-based incentives is one common approach, and it usually takes one of two forms. Bonuses are offered to individuals based on assessments of their performance, or bonuses are offered as salon wide incentives.

Sometimes, these incentives work in ways managers intended them to. But there are ways in which these methods of performance pay can backfire, causing contentious behaviours among employees, complaints about unfair pay distribution, or overwork and stress.

Rewards, by their nature have a punitive effect because they are manipulative. "Do this and you'll get that" is not really very different from "Do this or here's what will happen to you."

In the case of incentives, the reward itself may be highly desired; but by making that bonus contingent on certain behaviours, managers manipulate their subordinates, and that experience of being controlled is likely to assume a punitive quality over time, especially if the reward is always out of reach.

Punishment and reward are actually two sides of the same coin. Both have a punitive effect because they are manipulative.

Furthermore, not receiving a reward one had expected to receive, is indistinguishable from being punished. Whether the incentive is withheld or withdrawn deliberately, or simply not received by someone who had hoped to get it, the effect is identical. The more desirable the reward, the more demoralising it is to miss out.

The school of thought, which exhorts us to catch people doing something right and reward them for it, is not very different from the old school, which advised us to catch people doing something wrong, and threaten to punish them if they ever do it again. What is essentially taking place in both approaches is that a lot of people are getting caught. Managers are creating a workplace in which people feel controlled, not an environment conducive to exploration, learning, and progress.

Relationships among employees are often casualties of the scramble for rewards. Poorly designed incentive programs, and the performance appraisal systems that accompany them, may reduce possibilities for cooperation. If the bonus doesn't promote teamwork, your staff members will be pressuring the system for individual advantage. Instead of promoting the system for everyones benefit. The system will inevitably crash. In other words, without teamwork, there will be no quality performance or profit.

The surest way to destroy co-operation and, therefore, performance excellence, is to force people to compete for rewards or recognition or to rank them against each other.

For every winner, there are many others who carry with them the feeling of having lost. Therefore individuals in your salon environment need to have the same opportunity and the same benchmarks in order to keep the Status Quo. Never set-up a competition style system, where employees compete for a limited number of incentives or one prize. Recently I consulted with a salon who had put in place a competitive style bonus system, I don't know what the eventual outcome will be. It definitely won't be pretty, but four months in, the "team" is not very happy. The Bonus system is very simple, this is a good thing, that's probably the only good thing. All of the staff members compete for one prize. Simply, the staff member who generates the highest income each month, wins, and receives a whopping 25% of their gross income as a bonus. We already know that 25% of anything is too much, let alone gross income. I was certain, that this brainwave of a bonus system was pull out of a magician's hat, it definitely was not suggested by his accountant, or any other person who understands basic maths. I haven't even begun, this system goes even further, it absolutely, breaks every rule that relates to a bonus system.

If we overlook the financial shortcomings, and have a closer look, we'll find a few problems. Firstly, team motivation, the minute any stylist falls behind the leader, they stop trying, in fact, the same person has won the bonus competition each month, so no-one is motivated. Secondly, because they are all competing against each other, instead of focusing on self improvement, there is, no co-operation between any of the stylists. Thirdly, the team have been constantly complaining about how clients are being moved out of their column. The appointment book is continually changed, with clients being crammed in at busy times, customer service has started to degenerate. Next, one of the staff, who needed an income boost, started over charging his clients, one instance, amongst many that stood out, was a $15 Toner charged as an $80 Semi. The client never complained, but will the client return?

The internal manipulation of the system has bred dishonesty, bickering and mistrust. The whole team feels let down, those that get close to winning feel ripped off, and those who aren't in the race, have become unmotivated. This situation has evolved in less than five months. The owners problem now, is how to reverse and fix the problem. I believe he can't, without casualties, ie employees leaving. It's sad situation, because the intention was simply, to reward hard work. Again it's a case of you only know what you know, I'm sure if he had a more in-depth knowledge of bonus structures, and of what problems could be created, he would have chosen a different path.

BE WARY OF "MY TEAM"

Have you ever made the statement "my team are performing really well", then suddenly, the very next week you get a couple of resignations. There is a reason. The main reason is you don't have a team, you never had a team, and most importantly they were never "your team". They are employee's who are working for you, for a financial reward. They will only stay with you, as long as you offer them what they want. Exactly in the same way your clients treat your business. They will stay as long as you offer them what they want. They are not yours.

The definition of team is, a group brought together to perform a certain task within a certain time frame. Basically when the task is complete the team disbands. As employees come and go, the group dynamics in the salon change continuously. Occasionally the group will gel and you will have a happy productive group that become friends. This will go on for a while, then suddenly ,someone will leave to open their own business and others will follow, or leave to work in another salon.

Because "your team" is close knit, they keep in contact with each other, each one of them will play "the grass is greener game" and your salon will appear to be like a dead end job, even though it's probably not.

This happens everywhere, and it happens often, your job as a manager is to understand the group dynamics, then let it play out, control the outcome so you can get the most productive outcome for your business.

Each time a new staff member is introduced, or someone is promoted or moves up or down a level, the group will go through the four stages of group formation, in fact, this happens every time people get together, not just in the work place, and yes, I did say every time. No stage is missed, the development from one stage to another can be very quick, or take months or even stall at one of the phases, which can be very damaging.

THE FOUR STAGES OF GROUP FORMATION ARE:

- ◦ Forming
- ◦ Storming
- ◦ Norming
- ◦ Performing

FORMING:

The team meets and learns about the opportunities and challenges, and then agrees on goals and begins to tackle the tasks. In this stage team members tend to behave quite independently. They may be motivated, but are usually relatively uninformed of the issues and objectives of the team. Team members are usually on their best behaviour but very focused on themselves. Mature team members, begin to model appropriate behaviour even at this early phase. The meeting environment also plays an important role to model the initial behaviour of each individual. The major task functions also concern orientation. Members attempt to become oriented to the tasks, as well as to one another. Their discussion centres on defining the scope of the task, how to approach it, and similar concerns. Good management, using extensive orientation can set these goals and tasks in place very smoothly. To grow from this stage to the next, each member must relinquish the comfort of non-threatening topics, and risk the possibility of conflict.

STORMING:

This is the second stage of team development, where the group starts to sort itself out and gains each other's trust. This stage often starts when they voice their opinions and, as a result of this, a conflict may arise between team members as power and status are assigned or re-assigned.

When the group members start to work with each other, they start to learn about individual working styles, and what it is like to work with each other as a team. It also identifies different hierarchy of status, and of positions within the group. At this stage there is a positive and polite atmosphere, people are pleasant to each other, and they have different feelings of excitement, eagerness and positiveness, while others may have feelings of suspicion, fear and anxiety. The leader of the team, will then describe the tasks to the group, describe the different behaviours to the group and how to deal and handle complaints.

During this stage, participants form opinions about the character and integrity of the other team members, they feel compelled to voice these opinions, especially if they find someone shirking responsibility or attempting to dominate.

Sometimes, participants question the actions, or decision of the leader as the expectations become more defined.

Disagreements and personality clashes must be resolved before the team can progress out of this stage, and so some teams may never emerge from "storming," or re-enter that phase if new challenges or disputes arise. The duration, intensity and destructiveness of the "storms" can be varied. Tolerance of each team member and their differences should be emphasised, without tolerance and patience the team will fail. This phase can become destructive to the team, and will lower motivation if allowed to get out of control. Some teams will never develop past this stage; however, disagreements within the team can make members stronger, more versatile, and able to work more effectively as a team.

Managers of the team during this phase may be more accessible, but tend to remain directive in their guidance of decision making and professional behaviour. The team members will therefore resolve their differences and members will be able to participate with one another more comfortably. The ideal is, that they will not feel that they are being judged, and will therefore share their opinions and views. Normally tension, struggle and sometimes arguments occur. This stage can also be upsetting.

NORMING:

Resolving disagreements, and personality clashes, result in greater intimacy, and a spirit of co-operation emerges. This happens when the team is aware of competition, benchmarks, targets and service quality expectation. At this stage they begin to share a common goal. This is the unique time that all team members take the responsibility, and have the ambition to work for the success of the team's goals. They start tolerating the whims and fancies of the other team members. They accept others as they are, and make an effort to move on. The danger here is that members may be so focused on preventing conflict that they are reluctant to share controversial ideas.

PERFORMING:

With group norms and roles established, group members focus on achieving common goals, often reaching an unexpectedly high level of success. By this time, they are motivated and knowledgeable. The team members are now competent, autonomous and able to handle the decision making process without supervision. Dissent is expected and allowed as long as it is channelled through means acceptable to the team.

Managers and key senior stylists in the team during this phase are almost always participating. The team will make most of the necessary decisions. Even the most high performing teams will revert to earlier stages in certain circumstances. Many long-standing teams go through these cycles many times as they react to changing circumstances. For example, a change in leadership may cause the team to revert to storming as the new people challenge the existing norms and dynamics of the team.

FOUNDATION OF A SUCCESSFUL BONUS SYSTEM:

Although bonus Systems need to be based on profit and the reward may be in dollars, the targets should be based on performance. The more employees focus on their income, the less they will focus on satisfying their intellectual curiosity, learning new skills, or having fun, and those are the very things that make people perform best.

To begin with, you should put the employee bonus plan in writing. Your teams bonus plan is a document containing the details of the bonus program. The bonus program will not be of any use, and will not achieve the desired results, if it remains in the hands of the management

Base the bonus on results that are measurable or quantifiable. The rewards must be directly traceable to measurable performance standards

Be clear on WHAT, WHY, and HOW. Specifically, you have to be up front about what bonus is being given, why it is being given, and how the employees can get them, or what the employees should do in order to be entitled to the bonuses

Make sure, everybody gets something whenever the team exceeds expectation. In the spirit of fairness and providing equitable bonuses, the bonus should be structured in such a way that the lowest levels are easy to achieve. Doing this will ensure that everybody gets something, even if it is a minimal amount. More importantly, it will motivate the less performing ones to step it up and do better in order to get more bonuses in the future. Make the financial reward a strong enough incentive

1   From the business point of view, the bonus needs to be based on revenue (profit in dollars). Bonuses not based on revenue are ineffective, you cannot give what you have not collected. The entire team needs to realise that revenue must be collected to run an efficient business. You can calculate a monetary Target even if you use units sales or service benchmarks as your Staff Target.

2   The program must be easy to understand. If the bonus system is so complicated that team members cannot track their progress daily, the system will fail to have any motivating effect. At a staff meeting, explain how the bonus system will work before you implement it. Once it is in effect, in an employee only area, display a chart that tracks the team's progress toward their bonuses.

3   Many staff members tend to view a bonus, simply as extra pay that automatically comes their way. Thinking that a bonus will occur regardless of performance encourages a sense of complacency, hardly conducive to creating a more productive team. Team members must realise the bonus will only be earned when the set goals are met.

4   Tie the bonus to team performance. For a bonus system to be profitable, everyone must contribute. When the

Salon does well, then everyone does well. An effective bonus system can help create an even stronger team, while increasing job satisfaction for both the staff and management.

AN EXCELLENT BONUS SYSTEM. STEP BY STEP

Let's now, step by step, setup an excellent bonus system, that includes all of the features needed to make it successful. Of course, there are many excellent bonus systems, some are more suitable for your business than others. When you choose, or create your own, make sure it ticks all the following boxes.

1) The salon will have a minimum weekly income target, this does not include retail income.

2) Include a provision for bonus in your weekly target. A rule of thumb is about one dollar for each of your productive hours, If you are using the "pricing your services" APP add this in the drawings & dividends section of expenses. This will add about $1 to your prices. By doing this you can structure the bonus reward so it looks like this. "If you reach the target You will be paid $50-$100 plus 10-20% commission on the amount above your target". We will also include a 5% support staff bonus.

3) The Target Cycle would over a 4 week period, and the results averaged (divided by the number of weeks) so that a poor week can be offset with a better effort the next. A weekly

graph of the team results will be placed on the staff room notice board or handed out individually.

4) The Target for the bonus will be based on Unit sales. There should only be two or three categories. I would stick to my favourites, Chemical services, Retail units and Rebookings, 6 unit sales for every 10 clients serviced in each category. You can create other categories that may be more relevant to your business (NOT treatments), you might choose Facials, Massage or Cut & Blowdry. It doesn't matter so long as it improves your business, the only stipulation is that all must category targets be reached, and the Salon weekly income target must be reached.

5) For those who reached their target, we will share the bonus based on hours worked. All service income (not retail) above the Salon Weekly Target is included in the bonus calculation. This amount should never be above 20%, 10% is closer to the mark, remember we are also paying 5% to support staff, plus Superannuation. As an example; Assume that the minimum weekly income target is $10,000 and over the 4 week cycle the salon averaged $12,000, you will now have $8000 in your kitty Plus 4 weeks Provision lets say 4 x $100. Also assume that two individual made target, one of them works 40 hours per week and the other 10 hours per week. 15% of $8000 equals $1200 to be split between the two employees based on hours plus $400 provision for bonus in your price structure. The bonus payment would look like this:

- 40 Hour Employee, 15% is paid. $50 plus $960

- 10 Hour Employee, 15% is Paid. $50 plus $240
- Support Staff 5% of $1200 Paid. $60 each, this could be 3 or 4 apprentices. Receptionists should get their commission from retail sales, if all weekly targets are met.

Your cut, from the remaining Income, approximately $6690 plus $50 from the provision, remember that there are additional costs that will need to come out of what remains, but you would expect to end up with 40-50% of the $8000 as additional profit.

6) The bonus could be paid as, lump sum on week two of the next cycle or split into 4 weekly Payments. For impact a lump sum payment in front of other team members at team meeting will tick all the individuals ego and sense of achievement boxes. At this meeting you should debrief the results from the previous cycle. Highlight only the positives and refocus and assist, so the next cycle can achieve better results. DO NOT discuss individual winners, or individual failures, unless you want someone to resign. This must be a supportive meeting. Only discuss service milestones.The only reason you should make payment over four weeks would be to help your cash flow, if there a many recipients. Personally I favour the lump sum show. That's where the winner gets kudos.

THE ACTION PLAN

It's Time to make your decision

Are you a Hairdresser who has their own hairdressing salon?

Or

Are you a Business Person who operates a hairdressing business?

Dogged Self Belief

Driving your business forward does not require a super-intellect. Nor is there anything mystical about building a successful business.

Success is not based on luck. Calculating your costs, giving your clients value and setting your prices accordingly is a calculated winning formula.

Successful Business Owners are just ordinary people who have developed belief in themselves and what they do. Never, ever, admit your doubts, or suggest to others that you are not first class.

Perhaps the reason someone lacks the initiative and courage, is because they don't believe they are worth as much as they really are.

If you don't possess that dogged self belief your mind works against you, your streak of self depreciation begins to show in everything you do.

No one else can ever believe in you, unless, you show that you BELIEVE in yourself. Continued education, and the mastery of what you are taught, will go a long way to giving you the confidence to believe in yourself.

After reading this book I hope I have caused you to realise that your business, the market you're in, and your pricing strategy is ever evolving, and it often requires you to have a revolving door type approach.

Again to summarise your plan. Your first step, is to calculate your costs and add your margin using your APP, the seat time you calculate is the minimum you must charge to achieve your goals.

Make a list of all your competitors and find out all the things and services they offer that you offer, then find out all the things that they offer that you don't, include anything that you can think of that differentiates each business. Arrange your competitors in order, on a list, from most like your business to least, based on these findings. Place your salon in the appropriate place on this list. Next find out all of their prices.

Examine the prices of the Salons immediately above and below yours on the list, and see how your prices compare. If you are happy to be placed in this position in the market and you are happy with the value you give your clients all you need to do is keep an eye on these competitors and follow their prices, providing you are charging above your calculated seat time.

If your prices are lower than the salons immediately above and below yours on the list, devise a strategy to increase your prices and bring yours up to the market price. You will most likely need a combined approach, staff education, price restructuring, marketing campaign, added value, etc. Remember, you can attract market share if your prices are lower than your competitors, but don't advertise lower prices, make sure that you advertise to prospective clients that you provide better value or quality, they will do the price comparison, as your client base increases in small increments, regularly move your prices upward with a continued focus on value.

If your prices are higher than salons immediately above and below yours on the comparison list, you are in a good position, you still need a price strategy but you can take a softer approach. All of your marketing needs to focus on Skill, Quality, Value and Client Service. Even though you are in a good position your competitors have an advantage. If they emulate your service value or increase their offerings they could draw clients from you because of their same value at a lower price. In this situation, again, never mention price, only value and stroke your clients ego.

If you are not happy with your placement on the offerings list and you wish to raise your profile, set about introducing all of the client benefits that your competitors have and you don't. This may take some time, you may need new staff or upgraded skills with an education plan. You may need to refit your salon or change suppliers. You will also need a marketing campaign and a price rise strategy.

I've one last story, incase you are thinking a refit should be your first priority. When we purchased our first salon, it looked and felt pretty bad. There was old brown carpet on the floor, in the wet area, and yes, it was rotting and smelly. The salon had no air conditioning, we were upstairs with a tiny entrance to the street and no signage.

Our landlord was an absolute goose, we weren't allowed to install air conditioning, he was concerned that the wind might blow the 180kg cooling unit off the roof. We were not allowed to replace the carpet, because, he had chosen it and it was supposedly still new and very expensive. We couldn't place any signage on the building either, as the landlord lived in the flat next to us and feared too much traffic and noise from clients visiting us, even though we were in middle of a busy shopping strip. Despite these restrictions, by the end of our first year, we had moved from three staff to ten. On Saturdays we were so full, that clients were lining up the stairs and down the street in the hope of getting an appointment. Our prices were higher than anyone else in the area by a larger margin, they were inline with the best in Sydney.

We did eventually get the carpet replaced, we actually called the Health Department and dobbed ourselves in. We told them that the rotting carpet was a health risk and possibly illegal. The health inspectors were really good guys, they gave the landlord a mouthful, and, one week to replace the carpet with tiles in the wet area.

That old salon taught me heaps about providing what your clients value. The majority of clients, are not seeking the trendy ego trip, all they want is good old fashion service, high skill and a friendly, non threatening atmosphere.

I don't know how many times a new manager would tell us, the first thing they are going to do to improve the salon, is paint the walls. If we were employing a new manager, and they told us that they want to paint the walls, we didn't employ them, if they told us, they wanted to engage with our clients and make sure our business is delivering what the client wants, we immediately take them on. On it's own, coat of paint and groovy fixtures will change nothing, and attract no-one.

Why did that old salon have such success? Foremost, we placed a high value on education, every month all of our staff entered an IHS or Intercoiffure Competition, every other week we had formal training in the salon from a variety of sources. Our apprentices received over 900 hours of Cutting education during the four years of their apprenticeship, today apprentices who have only gone to college are lucky to receive 200 hours. We had a mentoring system in the salon and we constantly informed our clients about our intensive education.

We discriminated when we employed, we only employed happy, energetic, healthy, fit and enthusiastic people, who had a background of playing team sport. This discrimination might seem extremely tough and possibly illegal, it was, but my families future is on the line, not some politically correct do-gooder's.

At first it was almost impossible to find staff, but our reputation for excellence quickly grew. 9 out of 10 of our apprentices topped their classes at their Colleges.

To achieved our strict employment guidelines we met regularly with careers officers at all the local schools and implemented a really effective apprentice education system. On one intake we had 63 potential apprentices at the first meeting.

Because we weren't permitted signage at the front of our salon we had staff out on the street every day promoting our business. On the client value front, we were the first salon in our area to serve quality, freshly ground coffee, or offer complimentary wine, beer and refreshments.

The atmosphere in the salon was electric, the music appropriate, we only used and sold the most exclusive products, we had a real mystery. People wanted to know what was happening upstairs? Why were all those people lined up? Every Service had value added, everything was about giving our clients what they loved.

When you create a clear strategy, and move your prices in tandem with expanding client value and benefits, you will always be able to attract a constant flow of clients to your business, and charge a profitable price.

My best advice:

Outsource to professionals wherever possible.

Shift your mind set from Price to Value, don't let the price others charge dominate your service price.

Constantly review your Cost + Margin price, never charge below the seat time amount.

Focus everything on the client demographic that you want to attract, and on what those clients value, by continually surveying their needs.

Plan your price strategy for regular increases.

Comprehend, the cost of quality education is $0, as quality education returns one hundredfold.
"Cost = Return minus Price".

Set benchmarks that are relevant to your business, so that you can monitor improvement, don't compare your results to industry averages, if you are making a profit and improving your client numbers, that's enough.

Reward your employees for their efforts, but make sure all of them understand, and are in control of the reward system.

Believe in yourself and you will enjoy your journey.

www.ingramcontent.com/pod-product-compliance
Lightning Source LLC
Chambersburg PA
CBHW061247220326
41599CB00028B/5559